Social

COURAGE

Dr Eric Goodman, Ph.D., is a clinical psychologist, author, and speaker who specializes in helping people face their social fears and anxiety disorders. He has been a lecturer at Northeastern University and California Polytechnic State University. In addition to his private practice in San Luis Obispo, California, he runs Social Courage groups and retreats. When he is not busy 'scaring' his clients, he can be found scaring his three kids and patient wife.

Social
COURAGE

Coping and thriving with the reality
of social anxiety

Dr. Eric Goodman, Ph.D.

EXISLE
PUBLISHING

First published 2018

Exisle Publishing Pty Ltd
PO Box 864, Chatswood, NSW 2057, Australia
226 High Street, Dunedin, 9016, New Zealand
www.exislepublishing.com

A CiP record for this book is available from the National Library of Australia.

ISBN 978 1 925335 75 0

Designed by Nada Backovic
Typeset in 11.5/15.5pt Baskerville
Printed in China

This book uses paper sourced under ISO 14001 guidelines from well-managed forests and other controlled sources.

10 9 8 7 6 5 4 3 2 1

Disclaimer
This book is a general guide only and should never be a substitute for the skill, knowledge and experience of a qualified medical professional dealing with the facts, circumstances and symptoms of a particular case. The nutritional, medical and health information presented in this book is based on the research, training and professional experience of the author, and is true and complete to the best of their knowledge. However, this book is intended only as an informative guide; it is not intended to replace or countermand the advice given by the reader's personal physician. Because each person and situation is unique, the author and the publisher urge the reader to check with a qualified healthcare professional before using any procedure where there is a question as to its appropriateness. The author, publisher and their distributors are not responsible for any adverse effects or consequences resulting from the use of the information in this book. It is the responsibility of the reader to consult a physician or other qualified healthcare professional regarding their personal care. The intent of the information provided is to be helpful; however, there is no guarantee of results associated with the information provided.

To my spouse, Anya, and our children, Alex, Jessie, and Lana.

And to the family who, in their time of trauma and sorrow, gave me the gift of a kidney and a new life.

TABLE OF CONTENTS

Welcome to Social Courage

... Now, let's get to work!

If you are reading this book because you wish for social anxiety to no longer hold you back, then congratulations and welcome!

Reader, what are your thoughts about your social anxiety?

You may be thinking some of the following:

- Other people don't have to live with social anxiety on a regular basis, so why do I?
- Other people manage to get rid of their social anxiety, so why can't I?
- Social anxiety is a disease which this book should help me cure!
- Unless I eradicate my social anxiety, I will never achieve my social goals!

What if these thoughts were simply brain-noise? What if you no longer mistook these thoughts for facts? What if you are more than the sum of these thoughts? What if you no longer had to live your life based on this type of grumbling in your brain?

Most people who feel trapped by shyness or social anxiety will settle with the status quo and never seek help, be it from a knowledgeable therapist or from finding a scientifically based self-guided program and tackling it on their own. No, most people will go on suffering in silence and simply not have their social needs met. By reading this book you are taking a big step toward freedom from being controlled by anxiety. You are taking a step toward social courage.

WHAT IS SOCIAL COURAGE?

"Courage" is not a lack of fear. Courage, as that old cowboy John Wayne once said, is being afraid and saddling up anyway. "Social Courage" involves moving toward your social goals with your anxiety rather than waiting for the magical day when anxiety will vanish forever.

Now, I'm not suggesting that you are destined to *suffer* from social anxiety for the rest of your life. In this book you will learn tools for coping with socially anxious thoughts and feelings. What I am saying is that shyness and social anxiety are normal human experiences and that almost everyone experiences them to some degree in some situations.

What this book is NOT

Unlike many self-help books, I am not going to make unrealistic promises. I am not going to tell you that in ten weeks, your anxiety will be "cured"—or that, in those situations where you really wish you had zero social anxiety, you will have none. Social anxiety is a normal human experience—not a disease in need of a cure.

The purpose of this book

People who are struggling with high levels of social anxiety are typically stuck in a pattern that gives the anxiety power and control. I'd like for you to learn about this pattern so you can break it. I'd like for you to get unstuck and move forward with what is truly important to you. In short, I'd like for you to get free.

Freedom means accepting social anxiety as a normal human experience rather than an all-powerful force that can impose limits on you. Social anxiety has only as much power as you are willing to surrender to it.

The second main goal I have for you is to learn tools to help you minimize the sense of suffering that you experience while living with the reality of social anxiety. "Discomfort" in life is mandatory for us all. "Suffering" is something that people can take steps to minimize. It requires, however, a willingness to embrace, at least initially, even high levels of social discomfort. This is the most challenging part because it is counterintuitive. Instead of moving away from discomfort, which on the surface may *feel* reasonable, you must begin to move toward it—and with open arms.

It is my hope that this book can help you get free to pursue your social goals and minimize your suffering in the process. It won't take away all of your social anxiety … and that's actually a good thing! Now, before we get started, let's set some ground rules.

SOCIAL COURAGE GROUND RULES

1. Make this a priority

As this is a self-help book, it is up to you whether you read it or not and whether you do the exercises or not. You get out of this only what you put into it. What you put into it will directly relate to the priority in your life that you give it. You are free to stick with the status quo and not rock the boat. It will certainly be the more comfortable choice in the short term. Or, you could embrace the added discomfort of change in the short term so that you can win your freedom over the long term.

2. Consider making a "public" commitment

If you let someone know you are going to do something, then you are more likely to follow through. Tell someone you trust that you are taking concrete steps to move toward your social goals. This could be anyone, such as a parent, friend, spiritual advisor, therapist, or sibling … someone who will encourage rather than discourage you!

3. *Follow the program in order*

The material starts with the basics and builds up from there. I'd encourage you to go in order so that the foundational skills are in place. You certainly can skim or read the entire book first, but when it comes to implementing the program, I'd encourage you to start from the beginning and work up.

4. *Go at your own pace … but go*

You can go at whatever intensity level you'd like.

Working at a moderate pace, for most people, tends to lead to steady results that don't feel overwhelming. You certainly could progress through the challenges much more quickly and, if you manage to stick it out, make faster gains. Progressing through the program at a snail's pace will likely translate to gains at a snail's pace, but this is still movement in the right direction. It's your call.

5. *Be consistent*

Just keep at it, preferably doing some practice every day. Typically, it does not have to be a long practice, but just keep up with it. Any new thing worth doing is difficult at first, whether it is playing an instrument, learning a language, or changing your approach to social anxiety. It is new, awkward, and uncomfortable at times, but with a lot of practice, it gets easier!

6. *Be imperfect*

If you get bogged down in perfectionism (we will talk about this at length later in the book) you are defeating the purpose of the Social Courage program and will likely stay stuck. We are an imperfect species and the sooner you can embrace this, the sooner you will have more social freedom.

7. *Ask yourself if the time is right*

If you are in a crisis unrelated to social anxiety, feeling suicidal, have an active substance abuse problem, or have mental health or medical issues that need to be addressed, first seek appropriate professional help. You can read the book to see that there is hope for your social anxiety, but prioritize getting your life stabilized and then tackle the social anxiety with renewed vigor.

8. Be flexible

The tools presented in this book are taken from research demonstrating their effectiveness. These tools, which include acceptance, defusion, cognitive restructuring, compassion-focused interventions, and various behavior change strategies, have all been shown to be helpful. However, everyone is different.

Some tools may be particularly effective for you and others less so. Give them all a fair try and notice the ones that are most effective for helping you achieve your social goals while minimizing your suffering. In other words, if something is getting you where you want to go—do more of that rather than feeling like you need to have an equal emphasis on each tool.

Eileen

Eileen lived alone after her husband of forty years passed away. He was a gregarious man with many friends he met and maintained through his various social and charitable activities. Eileen had met her social needs through her husband and parenting their three children, who had since grown up and moved away to other parts of the country. She had never been one to put herself out there socially. She avoided social situations because she blushed at times and was terribly self-conscious about what people thought of her when they saw the crimson flush settle across her face.

PROGRAM OVERVIEW

Chapter 1 and Self-Assessment: Social Anxiety Is Normal

This provides you the opportunity to look at areas in your life negatively impacted by social anxiety or social avoidance. You have a huge decision to make—do you continue with things as they are, or do you change things in a way that moves you toward your social goals? After taking the assessment, if you decide to keep things as they are, then so be it. However, if you decide that social anxiety has exerted too much control over your life, you can take steps to propel yourself forward.

Chapter 2: When Normal Anxiety Turns Phobic

There is normal social anxiety and there is phobic social anxiety. Before taking action, you can learn about coping with normal anxiety while minimizing the disordered type. You can begin to understand the patterns and traps that lead to disordered anxiety in order to get unstuck and choose a new direction. You will learn how social anxiety impacts your (1) thoughts and beliefs, (2) emotional responses to social situations, and (3) your patterns of social behavior and avoidance. This will allow you to make a personalized strategy for coping with social anxiety while progressing toward your social goals.

Chapters 3–4: CBT 2.0 and Brain Noise

The mind can be a noisy place when you are feeling socially anxious. These chapters will help you learn ways to respond to this "brain noise" that will put it in perspective and limit its power to control you. Sometimes socially anxious beliefs can be directly challenged or altered. Other times it is a matter of learning to let the noise play on in the background while you avoid getting hooked by the content of unhelpful thoughts.

Chapter 5: Clean vs. Dirty Social Discomfort

The most unhelpful things you can do when feeling socially anxious are to try to force the feeling to go away or to get mad at yourself for simply having those feelings in the first place. Instead, you will learn strategies to help keep the socially anxious feelings from getting in the way of achieving your social goals. Additionally, you will learn ways to cope with those feelings that are present while minimizing suffering in the face of those feelings.

Chapter 6: Leaving Your Social Comfort Zone

Certain behaviors increase social anxiety and inhibit your life. You will learn to behave in ways that move you forward toward your social goals. This involves experimenting with new behaviors that challenge incorrect social beliefs, engaging in social exposures in order to practice coping effectively and building up your "social anxiety tolerance muscles," and identifying and moving toward your social goals step by step.

Chapter 7: Troubleshooting Social Anxiety

Finally, you will read about common ways people get stuck on their road toward Social Courage. Then it will be up to you to decide whether to press forward—one step at a time—understanding that you will stumble at times. You can learn from those stumbles and keep moving forward. In the end, no book, therapist, guru, or deity can transform your life if you are not willing to place one foot in front of the other.

This books aims to serve as a map to finding greater social freedom and I encourage you to take this journey. Go at your own pace ... but go.

1

Social Anxiety Is Normal

~~~~~~

Learn where social anxiety comes from and assess its impact on your life

Ethan

In his younger years, Ethan had completed two tours of duty in the Marines. He was battle-hardened and tough-as-nails ... except when it came to public speaking.

Now he found himself in a large, tightly packed room, getting called up on stage to accept an award in front of three hundred of his fellow small-business owners. He felt paralyzed with worry.

What if I open my mouth to give my speech and nothing comes out?

What if my legs don't stop shaking?

What if I blush—or worse, cry?

He had managed to stay away from public speaking in the past. In high school, he always chose to write a paper rather than do a class presentation. In college, he'd carefully selected the courses and professors that did not require public speaking.

> Now it was unavoidable. The host of the event had just called him up on stage, and the spotlight and all eyes were pointed directly at him. Heart pounding and mouth and throat bone-dry, he tightly gripped his note cards and slowly marched up to the stage.
>
> It was time!

Social anxiety is normal. It's not just you and it is neither your fault nor a sign of weakness.

If you are human, it is safe to assume that you, at times, experience social anxiety. You may feel that social anxiety makes you wrong, broken, or defective. Instead, I'd like for you to think of social anxiety as your birthright. Rather than it setting you apart from your fellow humans, it is actually something that ties you together within the broader human race.

Social discomfort, to some degree in some situations, is normal. In my entire life, I have met only one person with zero social anxiety. Let me tell you about him.

Carl

Carl was a fascinating middle-aged man that I had the pleasure of meeting when I was training to be a psychologist. He did not care in the least what other people thought about him. As a result of his genuine lack of concern about social rejection, he had absolutely no social anxiety whatsoever. He simply did not care.

Carl lived alone in a tiny apartment in Boston. He never pursued a career. He had no desire to impress people with the typical gadgets, trinkets, and doodads that most of us work hard to accumulate. He didn't care. He owned one ripped, gray T-shirt that he wore daily and never washed. So what! He couldn't smell the stink anymore and certainly didn't think about other's judgments. He didn't care. He owned one pair of pants, a matching pair of ripped grey sweat pants. When he was out and about and felt the call of

nature, he'd simply pee in his pants. After all, who did he have to impress? *He did not care.*
This is what zero social anxiety looks like.

Do you still want to completely get rid of your social anxiety? Would you trade places with Carl if it meant you would have zero social anxiety for the rest of your life?

No? Me neither. Social anxiety is part of the cost we pay for being part of a human community.

Social anxiety is only considered a problem if it:

1. negatively interferes with your social or life goals or activities.
2. causes excessive suffering.

If social anxiety, for example, were to prevent you from getting up on stage and performing a Broadway musical in front of a thousand people, this is only a problem if you are a professional performer who passionately wishes to be able to get up on stage and perform. The terror of getting up on stage and prancing around dressed like a cat while singing your heart out is not problematic if you are just an audience member attending the performance. If you cannot attend the show because of fears of being in the crowd, however, and you would love to be able to subject your spouse to an evening of singing felines, then it might just be a problem.

The thought of bungee jumping terrifies me. My fear of plummeting from a high bridge toward the rocky ground below while trusting my safety to a glorified rubber band wrapped around my ankle, however, only earns the status of a "problem" if my life's ambition is to take a job as a bungee instructor (which probably has its ups and downs).

BREAKING NEWS: SOCIAL ANXIETY IS NO LONGER A DISEASE!

Yes, that's right. Social anxiety, shyness, and even introversion are not diseases. In fact, they are perfectly normal human experiences.

Much of my professional life, however, is spent working with teens and adults who are extremely concerned about their social anxiety. Most of them are wishing for the day when their anxiety leaves them in peace so that they can carry on with life. They are waiting until it feels comfortable and anxiety-free to venture out into the world of friendship, job interviews, dating, and so forth.

They are waiting for a day that is likely never going to come. Social anxiety is normal.

As children, we go through a period of very intense stranger anxiety, where we "shy away" from all but those adults with whom we have learned to be comfortable over time. Long lost Aunt Bertha would come for a holiday visit, see us, and dive right in, ready to smother us with hugs and kisses. What did we (and countless other little ones) tend to do in the face of such an intimidating onslaught? We likely latched onto our parent's legs and looked away … occasionally sneaking peeks to see if the threat had vanished. In fact, mental health professionals are often *more* concerned when young children display no social hesitation in the presence of new adults.

But isn't that supposed to go away when you get older?

While most of us do feel less socially anxious as we get older, almost all of us remain socially hesitant or downright uncomfortable in at least some situations. It is a normal reaction and, to some degree, may even be necessary for living in a community of fellow humans. (Remember Carl?)

If you look at social anxiety as simply consisting of the expected presence of prickly feelings and thoughts, at least to some degree in certain social situations, maybe it does not need to seem like such a powerful and malevolent force. Rather than seeing social anxiety as a demon haunting you, perhaps you could begin to see it as a lifelong, albeit occasionally annoying, companion in life. This companion has no real power to hurt you, though your response to anxiety can make things go from normal anxiety to phobic anxiety.

SELF-ASSESSMENT

Without the pressure that you have to show this to anyone, take a few minutes and complete a self-assessment of the impact social anxiety has on your life (though we'll learn later in the book that it is really the struggle against social anxiety that causes the problems).

Below are some common social challenges and situations. These include both interpersonal experiences (tasks involving interacting with other people) and performance-based experiences (tasks where you feel like you are "in the spotlight"). Some people are highly triggered by only a few of the activities while others may be triggered by many.

As you look over the list, think about the following:

- Which activities or situations do you feel limited from participating in, at least some of the time, due to social anxiety?
- In which situations do you experience excessive suffering due to social anxiety?
- If you have never attempted these activities, imagine if you had the opportunity to attempt them.
- Also, imagine that for each of these activities, you had to be completely sober and not rely on specific friends, family, or objects (for example, staring at your cell phone at a party) to comfort you during the activities.

Check all that apply to you.

Interpersonal Situations	Anxiety Interferes
Meeting new people	
Making friends	
Deepening or maintaining friendships	
Dating	
Deepening or maintaining a romantic relationship	
Going to a party	
Hosting a party	
Making small talk	
Disagreeing with someone	
Directly asking for what I want	
Saying "no" to people when you want to	
Talking to your boss, teacher, other "authority figures"	
Attending a job interview	
Talking on the phone	
Talking to people I know only a little or not at all	
Inconveniencing others	
Asking for a favor	
Making eye contact	
Self-disclosure	
Other interpersonal situations that are triggers for me:	
Performance Situations	
Public speaking	
Speaking up in class or in a meeting	
Exercising in public	
Using public restrooms	

Showing up to places late	
Taking a test	
Being observed while working, writing, or eating	
Making a mistake (for example, giving a wrong answer, dropping or spilling something, tripping, or mispronouncing a word)	
Introducing yourself to others in a group	
Telling a joke	
Other performance situations that are triggers for me:	

IS YOUR SOCIAL ANXIETY A PROBLEM?

No one but you can honestly answer that question. It is easy, however, to fool yourself into settling for less in life in order to avoid social anxiety triggers. Rather than venturing out into uncomfortable social situations (and poking the social anxiety bear in the process) you might try to convince yourself that you are happier or better off without dating, friendships, and so forth—but are you only trying to fool yourself?

Social anxiety is a problem when it interferes with your life—when it calls the shots instead of you. When social anxiety robs you of your ability to do what you really want to do and it makes you suffer—then you are likely dealing with a condition known as Social Anxiety Disorder, which essentially is phobic social anxiety.

People can experience phobic social anxiety in just one or two areas such as public speaking or dating. Others experience phobic social anxiety as a more general fear of rejection from other people in many situations.

EXERCISE: What is the true impact of your social anxiety on your life?

Take a moment and write down all of the things that social anxiety has taken from you. How has it impacted (or prevented) relationships (family, friends, romantic interests, coworkers, and so on), education or career, fun, and freedom in your life? Please be specific—and honest with yourself!

How has social anxiety limited you in your life? What other areas of your life does social anxiety negatively impact? What might you miss out on in the future if nothing changes?

Another way to think about this is to imagine that you woke up tomorrow and magically your social anxiety no longer held you back in any way. How would your life be better? What activities would you then choose to do that you are not currently doing?

Remember, this is just between you and this book, so be honest with yourself. No one else has to know.

If you have given an honest assessment of the impact of social anxiety on your life, you may have accumulated quite a list. It might make you feel sad or frustrated just to look at it.

Preston

Preston was both a top-notch Silicon-Valley computer-programmer and gaming max-level Mega-Wizard. Technology, computers, and fantasy had been his entire life—and he got paid well for doing what he loved. His life outside of his computer screen, however, was minimal at best. While quite popular among members of his online gaming group, a motley band of elves and orcs, he had no friends outside of that group. He had never been to a party that was not a family event, and had yet to date. He had always assumed that if he worked hard in college and got a high-paying job, friendship and romance would somehow follow. Eight years later, it still hadn't.

The weekend of his brother's wedding was a real wake-up call. He felt painfully awkward and nervous meeting and interacting with so many people at the various functions. On top of that, he found himself uncomfortably jealous of his brother's social and romantic success.

Then the worst thing he could think of happened— during the wedding party, he was suddenly pulled up on stage by his tipsy mom who grabbed the microphone, introduced him as the "groom's brother who would like to make a speech!". She handed him the microphone, the room went silent, and the spotlight was upon him. Panicked, he managed to squeak out a few terrified words and fled the stage quickly, then hid in his hotel room the rest of the evening. *Something definitely had to change!*

Here's the list Preston made that lonely Saturday night.

The Impact of Social Anxiety on My Life:
- I don't have any close friends
- I have never dated

- I don't do a lot of fun things offline
- I can't public speak (and that will greatly limit my career progress)
- I don't go to the gym anymore because I'm worried what people there will think of me
- I don't go out to restaurants
- I don't travel
- I'm drifting further apart from my family
- I feel very lonely

You can learn to cope and thrive with social anxiety ... even though you may not believe it to be possible!

If you are like many people whose lives have been limited by social anxiety for a long time (maybe your whole life), you may not believe things can improve. I imagine that many of the people reading this book on some level are doubtful that the words on these pages could possibly offer anything that could truly help make their lives better. I'm going to ask you to set that belief aside for a bit and do the best you can to read on with an open mind. Just let that old belief be in the background without clinging to it for now. You can choose to reconnect with the "nothing-could-possibly-help thought" any time you wish.

TURNING PROBLEMS INTO GOALS

Just imagine for a moment: What if things could improve? I'd like you to try to open up to that idea for a moment. What if social anxiety no longer had the power to stop you from doing what you want? What if you could pursue your social goals and not be tortured by anxiety in the process? How would your life be different?

Review the list you just made of the ways in which social anxiety negatively impacts your life. Let's turn this around. What if these became your new goals?

Preston's List of Problems into Goals:

The Impact of Social Anxiety on My Life	My Goals
I don't have any close friends	I will take steps toward making new friends and deepening my relationships with work colleagues
I have never dated	I will take steps toward dating
I don't do a lot of fun things offline	I will plan at least one fun (and social) event each week
I can't public speak	I will learn and practice public speaking skills
I don't go to the gym anymore because I'm worried what people there will think of me	I will renew my gym membership and exercise there three times a week
I don't go out to restaurants	I will go out to eat at least once a week
I don't travel	I will take at least two trips each year
I'm drifting further apart from my family	I will call my parents and brother once per week and visit them during the holidays
I feel very lonely	I will take small steps daily toward my social goals

Notice that Preston is setting realistic goals that are amenable to breaking down into concrete steps and relying on his own actions and decision-making. He has control over whether he puts in the work needed to obtain these goals.

Goals that are less realistic would include items such as: I'll ...

... become an extroverted life-of-the-party who is adored by all

... have supermodels battling for my affection

... have the highest paying job in the world, but only work every other Tuesday

And equally implausible:

... I'll be perfectly comfortable in every social situation

While anything is possible, I would recommend focusing on more realistic goals—those that you have some control over obtaining.

EXERCISE: Now it is your turn. Take each of the items that social anxiety is negatively impacting and change them into realistic goals to work toward.

My Goals

The Impact of Social Anxiety on My Life	My Goals

Am I willing to go on this journey? Is it worth it?

Even though it looks more hopeful to see a list of goals than problems, it still may seem quite daunting to take on social anxiety in order to achieve these goals.

Making any changes in life can be challenging. There is always the alluring siren call of the status quo gently lulling us into complacency. Learning to move toward uncomfortable social situations that may not only seem challenging, but truly scary at times, really gets those sirens singing. Those anxiety sirens would probably like you to put this book down right now; surely there is an e-mail to be checked or a show to be binge-watched. Anxiety certainly doesn't want you to rock the boat!

So, the key question for you right now is:

If it were possible for you to achieve your social goals, would it be worth it for you to work hard in order to earn those rewards? It is important to understand that I am also talking about increasing your social risk. There is no courage without risk. Staying home alone night after night wrapped in a blanket of distraction and complacency will surely minimize your social risk. Likewise, however, it will minimize your social rewards in life. Will you choose to go down the road of courage or complacency?

Are you willing to not only work hard, but also increase your social risk if it means achieving your goals?

If your answer is YES:

Plan on spending some time every day continuing with this book and working toward your goals. The first step will be to learn more about social anxiety disorder and how to more peacefully coexist with normal social anxiety while discarding the "disordered" part.

If your answer is NO:

There are many reasons why you might say no. Perhaps there is something else in your life more pressing right now (depression, illness, addictions, relationship crisis or abuse, final exams, and so on). That is okay—address what you need to and then you can rethink your goals at a later time. You can still continue to read this book and get a better understanding of what increasing your social courage would look like. You might even decide to move toward your social goals, but at a significantly slower pace. That's okay too. It's your life and only you can set your own priorities. Perhaps progressing at a slower pace now will lead to faster momentum later on. It is okay to simply dip your toes into the pool of social courage, moving forward very slowly, while understanding that gains will likely be at a snail's pace until you decide to invest yourself further into your own forward momentum.

WHY WE EXPERIENCE SOCIAL ANXIETY

Bob and His Brain

Bob took his brain for a walk with him one cool fall afternoon. His brain chatted pleasantly with him about the delicious cup of coffee they were consuming when suddenly they saw someone walking toward them. "Is that person a threat?" his brain vigilantly inquired. As the person neared and Bob's brain got a closer look, he realized that danger was unlikely. They went back to enjoying the coffee and the pleasant chirping of the birds overhead. As a small group of teens walked in his direction, his brain once again jumped to attention and demanded to know, "Are those people threats?" As the group walked on by, the threat level rapidly diminished. And so Bob and his brain continued on their journey, Bob enjoying his coffee and the sunny afternoon while his brain did what it thought best in order to keep them both alive.

When I explain that social anxiety is normal, I am often asked why we experience so much of it. People want to know, "Where does it come from?"—hoping that by understanding its origins, it will make facing social challenges easier.

There are many reasons why you experience social anxiety in the normal course of human interactions. Is it nature or nurture, hardware or software, biology or bullies, temperament or teaching? Yes, all the above!

Let's start at the beginning.

Ancestral Inheritance

Early humans and pre-humans lived in very dangerous times. They existed in small tribes and spent their time hunting and gathering food, while avoiding becoming the food of other wild animals that would frequently hunt them. Resources could be scarce and members of other tribes were willing to kill in order to acquire those precious resources for their tribes. If you wandered off during a hunt and happened upon a hunter from another tribe, it was often a kill-or-be-killed situation. Strangers were in fact very dangerous. Coming across a member of another tribe would have naturally triggered a fight-or-flight response and all of the panicked dread that comes with that. Fear of strangers would have been life preserving.

In your own small tribe, your options for mates would have been limited. Asking that lovely cave-person out for a jungle romp may have been a high-pressure situation. If they turned you down, your mating pool suddenly seemed very limited and texting the cutie in the neighboring clan was a little ways off. Given the biological imperative to procreate and spread your genes, anxiety around rejection seems reasonable to some degree.

It would have also made sense for these early ancestors of ours to develop a "better safe than sorry" nervous system.

Grog and Trog

One afternoon, a couple of the younger members of a small tribe, Grog and Trog, noticed something moving far down in the valley below. Grog's brain told him that surely it must be a tasty bunny rabbit, and he ran down into the valley to kill it. Trog's brain, on the other hand, wasn't so sure. It presented Trog with a high-definition thought that the moving object might be a ferocious saber-toothed tiger, so he anxiously decided to hold back and wait for the other hunters in his tribe to return before pursuing it together—with spears sharpened. Maybe nine times out of ten, it turns out to be a delicious bunny, but on the tenth time Grog got eaten. Erring on the side of anxiety actually kept Trog alive and therefore increased the chances that he will spread his DNA (and his cautious ways) to future generations. The Grogs of the world may have been weeded out.

In other words, humans may have evolved the tendency for anxiety right from the start.

Temperament

Let's say you went into a day care center to visit your child, who is sitting quietly on the carpet with her class listening to the teacher read a story. You quietly sneak in so that you can watch your little angel without making a disturbance. As luck would have it, however, you inadvertently bump into a shelf, knocking down a stack of metal bowls and creating a startling BANG in the process! The group of surprised children will react in a wide variety of ways. Some may cry from the sudden adrenaline surge, some will look over with concern, some will casually peek at the teacher to see that everything is okay, and a few may be barely disturbed by the commotion, or even giggle in response.

When it comes to temperament, you get the nervous system you get. Some people are simply born with a more hair-trigger nervous system than others. Their fight-or-flight system gets activated much more easily and to a higher degree. On the other end of the spectrum are people whose nervous systems take much more intense stimuli to evoke a nervous reaction. These people might be found among daredevils, test pilots, astronauts, Fortune 500 CEOs, and sociopaths.

These temperamental differences influence our levels of social discomfort. Some of us are just born to be "slow to warm up" to new people or social situations. There is no need to condemn yourself for an attribute that was not of your selection. Rather, you can do the best you can with what you are given—it is normal for you. Even pervasive social anxiety may come with its own positive and desirable attributes such as empathy, compassion, and thoughtfulness.

We've known for quite some time that genetics play a role in temperament. The genetic code you inherit from your ancestors plays a significant role in how your own nervous system responds to the environment around you. However, more recently we have learned of a fascinating phenomenon called epigenetics, which demonstrates that not only do you inherit genetic code, you also seem to inherit ways in which that genetic code is expressed, based on the experiences of your recent ancestors.

In other words, what happened to your ancestors can impact you! If your grandmother lived in times of food scarcity or starvation, your body may want to store more fat. Grandmother mice in labs that are trained to have phobias of a particular scent have grandchildren that fear that same scent. It could be that you can experience social inhibition based on social experiences that you never even directly had. This notion of epigenetic inheritance is a new and exciting development in science research.

The bottom line is that you do not get to pick your temperament (or the things that happened to your ancestors), but your temperament can play a huge role in your level of social comfort or discomfort. Not your choice and not your fault—and, there are advantages to having an anxious temperament.

While people with hair-trigger nervous systems may be more uncomfortable (or at least more revved up) initially in novel social situations, they also may find more delight in a good meal, a sunset, or a pleasant conversation with a friend. They may simply feel things more strongly, even the pleasurable things. I've heard it likened to being more alive than someone with a low-arousal nervous system. People with an anxious temperament have the nervous system of a souped-up sports car! For people with low-arousal nervous systems, they may be in their element when thrill seeking or corporate-ladder climbing, but day-to-day living can be incredibly dull.

Learning

No matter how much of your anxiety is hard-wired through temperament, you learn to feel social anxiety in certain situations based on your own experiences in life. This learning takes place from both direct and indirect experiences.

Directly learned social anxiety may come from events such as:

• Experiencing rejection, despite your best efforts (happens to all of us at some point to some degree!)

- Being bullied
- Being the subject of laughter for a social mistake (dramatically slipping on the ice in the winter, anyone?)
- Being picked on for a flaw in appearance or social skill deficit
- Being picked on for being different (aren't we all different from some people?)

I worked with a man in his mid-sixties who had carried a lot of social anxiety and sense of shame with him since childhood. When asked about his rejection history, he could only recall one event that had really stuck with him and, unfortunately, had set the social tone for his entire life. He had been giving a presentation in front of his class and had lost his train of thought and could not continue. He recalled the experience as if it had happened yesterday: "They all laughed at me!" This event that had retained so much power over him had taken place sixty years earlier—in kindergarten! He had hidden from countless social opportunities throughout his life in order to avoid being on the receiving end of what he feared would have been brutal rejection. In fact, he could not recall a time at any other point in his life when he experienced a "significant" rejection.

I would encourage you to consider working toward forgiving yourself and others for the childhood rejections that so commonly occur. Let them remain in the past and move toward greener social pastures.

Occasionally, I come across people who continue to receive a steady stream of rejection, even as adults. This may occur for reasons such as feeling trapped in an abusive relationship or a lack of adequate social skills for a particular context. It is not surprising that this may come with a higher level of social anxiety. We will talk later in the book about what to do when your social fears do come true.

Indirectly learned social anxiety comes from other sources such as:

- Having a parental figure who models either social anxiety-related avoidance or social rejection of others
- Seeing others experience rejection (for example, a speaker getting heckled)

- Observing the destructive work of social media "trolls" (people who spread hate and rejection with sadistic enthusiasm across the spectrum of the internet)
- Other media forms

The media influences social anxiety in a number of ways. First, when public figures are caught on camera being imperfect, whether it is an unfortunate quote taken out of context, dressing unfashionably in "mom jeans," or melting down in the midst of a stressful day, it can become breaking news and repeatedly splashed across newspapers, television, and the internet expanse for millions to see. That certainly ratchets up the social pressure for public figures and fuels vicarious fears among the socially concerned everywhere—*What if it happens to me?! I'd better be careful, or else.*

Second, you are constantly exposed to stereotyped social behavior in media portrayals. I recall as a child watching the nervous character of Alfalfa from *The Little Rascals* TV show giving a speech in class only to be the target of voracious laughter and derision from his elementary school classmates. It gave me the impression that public speaking was quite the risky endeavor. Watching other people be rejected in a particular situation may lead the viewers to have at least some social hesitation in those situations.

The media is also chock-full of socially "perfect" portrayals that are impossible for anyone in reality to consistently and successfully imitate. When you tune into a TV show or movie, you are not seeing real life. You are seeing professional models (genetic anomalies in themselves) who are decorated by a team of hair, wardrobe, and makeup specialists, then enhanced with special lighting and effects. Yes, their words come out smooth and flowing—they were written by a team of writers, memorized, and rehearsed repeatedly by professional actors, who are then given multiple takes in order to get it just right. This is a far cry from the awkward complexities of real-life social interactions. When you compare yourself to this, you are sure to feel that you are coming up lacking.

While I do not believe it is the intent of TV and movie producers to make you feel bad about yourself, advertisements are a whole other ballgame. The purpose of an advertisement is to generate a desire so strong that you will go out and take action. How do they try to do this? Unfortunately, marketers do this much of the time by crafting their ads to make you feel bad about yourself so that their product or service, once purchased, will make you better—at least until the next advertisement comes along to make you feel bad again.

As I write this, I am randomly selecting and flipping through an entertainment magazine from my office waiting room. Through big, bold, colorful pictures and large text, the ads I see send the following messages:

- You are a subpar parent, BUT, you can be an attractive, cool parent ... IF you purchase that Disney cruise for your next vacation!
- Hey, boring person, you can be fun, glamorous, and desirable if you head out to Las Vegas for your next vacation!
- As it is, your skin could scare small children and puppies, but could be radiant perfection in just sixty seconds if you purchase our product!

How many of these ads do you see in a day, week, month, year, or lifetime? You are force-fed a steady media diet of "not-good-enoughs," and these days, many of us are connected to these media messages every waking hour. If you are like most of us, your brain is stuffed full of thoughts and images of social threat from the daily all-you-can-eat buffet of targeted media messages. In a later chapter, we will talk a lot about ways to cope with this "brain noise."

In addition to commercial media, you are probably bombarded daily with social media messages from friends and family that can heighten your social comparison concerns. These messages are one-sided, typically, with people selecting only the most flattering photos (at least of themselves) to post. Subtly or not so subtly, they convey the message that they are eating the most desirable foods, dating the most desirable people, traveling to the most desirable locales, all the while laughing and smiling in a state of Nirvanic bliss. The takeaway message is often, *What the heck is wrong with you and your life?*

The problem is that you are again seeing a one-sided portrayal of the complexity that is human life. Underneath the social mask in the picture of the smiling "friend" is the jet lag, diarrhea, hangover, and the stress and pressure to have maximum fun which, of course, ends up dampening the fun. You most often don't learn of these facts through your friend's social media posts—they remain the hidden realities (that life is not perfect) that we all share, but few talk about openly. The message you receive over and over again is that if you are not perfect in every way, you should feel bad about yourself in relation to others. Social anxiety flourishes with the belief that these "flaws" of yours will become the target of social rejection and humiliation.

In addition to the social and commercial media's impact on your feelings of social wellbeing, the human population is spending less time interacting in person and increasingly more time turned inward on internet-connected devices. The probable result is that humans are and will likely continue to become increasingly uncomfortable in certain social situations requiring in-the-moment external interactions. Time will tell just what the social implications are for humanity, but it appears that things are and will be different. Increasing levels of social discomfort will likely become the new normal.

Other Contributing Factors

There are numerous other factors that may contribute to an underlying feeling of anxiety in social (or other) situations. I'm referring to the normal background anxiety thoughts and feelings that accompany us, at least from time to time, throughout our lives.

Stress is the perception of having more on your plate than your current resources can manage. It might be a real perception. If you have tasks in front of you that require four hours of work and they are due in two hours, stress often results. Stress then revs up your nervous system and when entering certain social situations, you might find yourself a bit more on edge compared to having gone straight from a relaxing day at the beach. You may also have noticed that lower levels of assertiveness—for example, saying "yes" to things that you do not want to do—can significantly increase stress.

Another thing that might rev up your nervous system is caffeine (which is one of my favorite things, but a reliable anxiety producer for many) and other stimulants. You may be surprised to read that things such as alcohol and marijuana that many people take to decrease their anxiety may also lead to increased anxiety at times. Additionally, many prescription and over-the-counter medications have increased anxiety as a common side effect. Some of these medications are used to treat medical conditions such as hyperthyroidism, blood sugar or neurological dysregulation—any of which can cause physical symptoms of anxiety to be present as well.

Besides stress and substance use, there are other lifestyle factors that can contribute to higher baseline anxiety levels. Take sleep. People are sleeping less these days. Getting too little sleep, among other things, can rev up the nervous system. People might feel tired, but wired. One of the reasons people may be sleeping less is the massive amount of time spent on screens. Many people are plugged into technology from the moment their iPad wakes them up in the morning until they fall asleep with it in their bed in the evening. So much technological stimulation must be having profound impacts on the human nervous system beyond diminished sleep quality and quantity. This is a reality for people and societies across the world. The times they are a-changin'.

We have known for many years that physical activity is one of the best stress, anxiety, and depression treatments known to humankind. With ever advancing technology, however, our species has become more sedentary and with it, one of the best tools for improving our baseline anxiety has increasingly been reduced.

Add to all of this other societal factors such as:

- Economic and job insecurity
- Focus on money and achievement as the measure of a person's value
- Racism, sexism, ageism, and other forms of discrimination
- The "war on terrorism" making daily headlines

- Normal culture-based time pressure to achieve certain milestones, such as education, career, marriage, children, promotion, and so forth, by certain ages

And, in the background of all of the above, is the challenge of dealing with normal aging and the knowledge of the inevitable end to our lives ...

I apologize if I have totally depressed you. My point in all of this is that there is a certain background anxiety that is normal, unavoidable, and universally experienced. The inevitable presence of anxiety in life was something the Buddha observed over twenty-five hundred years ago—and he didn't have to rush through the airport looking for an outlet to charge his smart phone so he could respond to a "critical" email before texting his spouse his revised flight schedule!

Yes, I do think society could benefit from some changes that would certainly reduce baseline anxiety levels, but while you wait for that to occur (hopefully not holding your breath) perhaps you could benefit from labeling a significant portion of your inner experience as normal rather than calling it an illness or heaping shame on yourself for simply observing that you too have these universal experiences.

At the same time, you can choose to make some changes in order to lower your baseline anxiety arousal. A common theme in this book is to accept what you cannot change, and change what you can.

EXERCISE: What could you change that would be helpful?

- Diet/Nutrition
- Exercise levels
- Substance use
- Sleep
- Stress management
- Other:

....

....

....

....

The Verdict: It's Not Your Fault!

As you can see, social anxiety is normal and unavoidable for almost all of us. You are not alone in this, though you may have felt alone with these inner experiences for quite some time. Since anxiety is and will likely remain a part of you (and most other people), you might as well take the pressure off yourself that you must get rid of it completely. Rather, you can begin to shift your focus from the eradication of a normal human emotion to pursuing your social goals while adapting to and coping with the anxiety you experience along the way.

But my social anxiety terrifies me. It does not seem normal to me!

When social anxiety turns "phobic," it is no longer run-of-the-mill anxiety. Rather, it is a process that may threaten to derail the social course of your life.

Fortunately, like all phobias, phobic social anxiety that has arisen can be successfully reversed, though "success" does not mean getting rid of the normal daily experience of social anxiety. It means learning to live more adaptively with social anxiety.

The first step toward dealing with phobic social anxiety is to learn about what makes and maintains a phobia and how to break out of the phobia cycle.

2

When Normal Anxiety Turns Phobic

Free yourself from the phobic cycle by understanding anxiety's secret rules

Alisha

Alisha has had a secret crush on Brandon since the fourth grade. Now it was prom night and he was on his way to pick her up. What if he didn't like her? What if she made a total fool of herself? She had never been on a date before and tonight she was quaking in her boots! She felt a twinge of nausea as she heard his car pull up. *What if my parents embarrass me?* She felt excited and anxious at the same time. Who knew dating could be so scary? Maybe she should just say she was ill (she certainly felt like it) and stay home where life was safe and comfortable. She crept down the stairs nervously. "Okay, I will do this!" she told herself, not quite believing it.

Brandon

Brandon drove slowly, dreading every second. He quickly glanced at his reflection in the rearview mirror. Still there! The large pimple on the end of his nose stared at him, mocking his evening plans. It would almost have been funny if it had not happened on prom night. *Alisha will not want to be seen with me, and who could blame her?* Sure, he'd had a crush on her since ... always—he just wasn't ready for this! He had been briefly jubilant when his friend had arranged this date, playing matchmaker. Now he was hating life and hating his friend even more! He turned onto her street and his heart beat wildly in his chest. He cranked the AC and sucked in deep breaths, which made him feel even more light-headed. His hands were moist with sweat. He knew he would need to make small talk with Alisha's parents, and how horrified they would be to see what an awkward loser their daughter had agreed to go to the prom with! The panic reached a jarring crescendo as he parked in front of her house. He sat paralyzed in his seat, sweat now dripping down his forehead. He continued to sit frozen in his car praying that none of this was real, wishing desperately to awaken alone in his bed where it was safe. His intestines suddenly came alive with a sharp ache and he fought back tears as he realized that he urgently needed to get to a bathroom!

WHAT IS PHOBIC SOCIAL ANXIETY?

For approximately one in ten individuals, normal social anxiety will grow into a phobia at some point in their life. This social phobia or social anxiety disorder, as it is commonly called, is not any different from other phobias (for example, an irrational fear of heights, snakes, or circus clowns) other than the particular content of the phobia, which in this case is interpersonal or performance situations.

The primary fear that people with a social phobia experience is that of rejection from others. The belief they tend to hold is that rejection is very likely to occur and the consequences are socially catastrophic. These beliefs then lead people to behave in avoidant ways that end up maintaining or increasing their social fears. In other words, the solutions that people with social phobias come up with to feel better are essentially those things that make the phobia stick around or get worse. When it comes to phobias, typically the impulsive "solution" IS the problem.

Due at least in part to the shame they feel, most people with a social phobia will never get treatment and are likely to remain trapped by anxiety throughout their lifetime. (By reading this book, you are one very big step ahead of this!) People who remain trapped by a social phobia often miss out on a lot that life has to offer. They tend to get married later or not at all. On average, they tend to go less far in their education and remain underemployed throughout their career. In many ways the course of their lives is determined by the limitations that social anxiety imposes upon them.

Some people develop a social phobia in one or two situations (for example, public speaking and dating) while others have more generalized social fears. We see social phobias across all walks of life and, in recent years, high-profile celebrities and athletes have courageously disclosed their own battles with phobic social anxiety. If you are struggling with a social phobia, you are not alone—it is the most common anxiety problem we humans experience!

Normal vs. Phobic Social Anxiety

Normal Social Anxiety	Phobic Social Anxiety
Scary social thoughts are floating around your consciousness, but not much credence or attention is given to them.	You are often hooked by these thoughts. You monitor them, believe them, and perhaps struggle with them. You change your behavior based on them.

Anxious feelings before or during a social event are seen as normal discomfort that "comes with the territory."	You are often locked in a battle to get rid of these feelings, which ironically tends to intensify them significantly.
You follow through with desired social plans, albeit uncomfortably at times.	You avoid social situations that are "triggers" when you can, and when you can't avoid them, you behave in ways to "minimize risk" that ironically increase anxiety in the long run.
You get your social needs met much of the time.	Your social needs are often not met.

In order to downgrade phobic social anxiety back to normal, run-of-the-mill social anxiety, the first step is to learn about how phobic social anxiety tricks you into behaving in ways that maintain or strengthen its hold over you.

PHOBIAS 101

When I didn't get a phobia

When I was ten years old, I was playing at my cousin's house when I saw their large black Labrador, Brooks, napping peacefully under a window. I loved dogs and quickly ran up to hug the sleeping animal. Brooks was startled by my playful embrace and proceeded to transform from angelic to ferocious in a micro-second, which scared me almost as much as the painful bite she delivered.

Afterwards, my brain told me, "Maybe dogs are dangerous and will hurt you if you don't keep your distance!" At that point, I was "at risk" for developing a phobia of dogs—but I did not, due to circumstances beyond my ten-year-old control.

I had a pet dog at home. In fact, I had always had a dog. When I went home that evening, my dog was thrilled to see me and I had the corrective experience of being safe around a dog. Likewise, my friends all had dogs, as did members of my large extended family. Within the weeks that followed, the dog bite began to seem only like a freak occurrence. A significant part of my life included having a dog nearby. The initial trepidation worked itself out as I had more and more positive, bite-free dog experiences.

I never developed a dog phobia.

When I did get a phobia

I do not think there has been a single year when I have not flown in an airplane. For the first nineteen years of my life, I saw flying as either a fun adventure or a convenient, yet often boring, way to get from point A to Point B. Turbulence during flights just meant I was rocked and lulled into a peaceful nap.

That all changed one dark and very stormy night at thirty thousand feet!

While studying abroad in college, I was on a flight from Beijing to Hong Kong and, as usual, I fell into a deep sleep. Suddenly I was violently shaken awake, not by the moderate turbulence that the flight was experiencing, but by my philosophy professor in the seat next to me.

"We're going to crash!" she exclaimed, shaking me harder. "The plane's going down!"

The plane was not going down. The good professor was having a severe panic attack, and through random happenstance my seat was next to hers. Initially I was startled, but after a quick glance around I noticed that everything seemed fine and then I quickly fell back to sleep—only to be shaken awake once again.

"We're not going to make it!" she told me as she squeezed my arm.

Again, sleep overtook my annoyance. The pattern repeated several more times during the flight, but I didn't think much about it afterwards.

> My next flight took place a month later. I was flying from Seattle to Kansas City and was seated next to my mother who has long been frightened of flying. Shortly after takeoff we hit some turbulence and my mom suddenly and anxiously squeezed my arm. I then found myself shaking with fear, bombarded by thoughts and images of the plane crashing.
>
> The terror I felt on that flight grew stronger with each subsequent flight I took! Little did I realize that I had begun behaving in ways that fueled a severe phobia that would last for a decade.

In both situations, I was at risk for developing a phobia. Being at risk is a combination of the following:

- Having experienced (either directly or indirectly) a safe situation (for example, poodles, flying, or small talk) as being a serious threat (getting bit, scary airplane experience, or humiliating rejection).
- The risk that the event will lead to a full-blown phobia increases based on other risk factors such as temperament and other early factors. (Did a parental figure overprotect you when you felt wary of something realistically safe? Did they model fearful avoidance?)

Being at risk for developing a phobia simply means that you feel extra cautious around a certain thing or situation. What you do with these cautious feelings will determine whether they grow into a phobia or not.

Turning these cautious feelings into a full-blown phobia

More important than understanding what causes these initial cautious feelings to emerge is understanding how people inadvertently grow them into a full-blown phobia. Once you understand this pattern, you can then learn to behave in ways that diminish the phobia's hold over your life. You can learn to break this pattern.

THE PHOBIA CYCLE

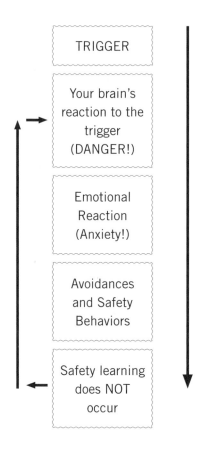

The lights dim as the music starts to play. Anxiety approaches you and enthusiastically tells you, "Let's dance!" Should you decline, then the tantrum begins—there's yelling, pleading, demanding, with a bit of seduction tossed in. It makes a convincing case and soon there you are again being led around the dance floor by anxiety. You feel trapped, stuck, and hopeless. You are doing the phobia dance! However, if you begin to understand the dance, you can take the lead. You can change the dance and begin to regain control.

CARE AND FEEDING
OF A PHOBIA

Step 1: Trigger

An anxiety "trigger" can be anything that is reasonably safe, but you have learned to be unreasonably afraid of. They can be particular people, places, things, situations, memories, body sensations, and so forth.

Brandon's List

- Girls
- Parties
- Crowds
- Public Speaking
- Intestinal Discomfort
- Pimples
- Sweating
- Conflict
- Talking on the phone
- Looking imperfect
- Using public bathrooms

EXERCISE: Let's look at those triggers that tend to increase your social anxiety. Write as many of your triggers as you can come up with below:

....

....

....

....

....

....

....

....

....

....

....

....

....

....

....

....

....

Step 2: Your brain interprets the trigger as dangerous

The human brain is an interpretation machine. Late at night, alone in the dark, you hear a noise outside your door. Your brain will want to know exactly what made that sound. Is it an intruder, your child sneaking into the kitchen for a midnight cookie raid, the wind, or a ghost? Your brain will try to come up with an explanation that you can believe.

When it comes to other people and social or performance situations, your brain will try to decide for you whether the situation is socially safe or socially dangerous (or somewhere in between).

Let's look at Brandon's triggers and his brain's corresponding interpretations.

Brandon's Triggers and Interpretations

• Girls	Girls will reject and humiliate me—they'll think I'm a joke.
• Parties	No one will want me there. I'll be the outcast.
• Crowds	They'll see what a loser I am. I will be ridiculed.
• Public Speaking	I will sweat profusely and I'll never live it down.
• Intestinal Discomfort	I will have to rush to a bathroom or might poop my pants.

•	Pimples	People will think I'm disgusting—they'll laugh at me.
•	Sweating	If people see me sweat, they'll think I'm a disgusting loser.
•	Conflict	If someone doesn't like me, I can't handle it.
•	Talking on the phone	I'll embarrass myself—I'm terrible at it!
•	Looking imperfect	If I don't look perfect, people will judge me very harshly.
•	Using public bathrooms	If people hear me using the bathroom, I'll be humiliated.

Ultimately, Brandon's brain presents him with interpretations of his triggers that relate to a high probability of humiliation and rejection from fellow members of our species. These are the same danger interpretations as being in a plane that might crash or being confronted by a dog that may attack. Social rejection is a danger interpretation because, like it or not, humans are pack animals. The thought of being ridiculed, rejected, or otherwise being placed apart from your community IS anxiety provoking. Remember what happens to animals shunned by their herds in the wild—they become snacks for predators! We have a strong need to be connected with other people and become very concerned when such human connection is threatened.

EXERCISE: What automatic danger interpretations does your brain make in the face of your social triggers?

....

....

....

....

....

....

....
....
....
....
....
....
....
....
....
....
....
....
....
....
....
....
....
....

Step 3: Automatic emotional reaction

Public speaking, parties, assertiveness, conflict, dating, small talk, or even rejection are NOT what causes you anxiety. It is when your brain interprets the situation as a threat (a "danger interpretation") that anxious feelings naturally emerge in those situations—or even at the anticipation of entering those situations.

Let's use an example of the presence of a dog in order to see how differently people feel based on their brain's interpretation of the situation.

Person 1 is walking down the street and sees a labra-doodle dog approaching. She automatically interprets the situation as:

"What a cute, friendly dog!" Then she feels happy and wants to pet it.

Person 2 is walking down the street and sees a labra-doodle dog approaching. She automatically interprets the situation as:

"Oh, that dog reminds me of my dog that was kills by a car last month ... I really miss her!" Then she feels sadness or grief.

Person 3 is walking down the street and sees a labra-doodle dog approaching. She automatically interprets the situation as:

"That's the good-for-nothing dog that keeps pooping in my yard!" Then she feels anger.

Person 4 is walking down the street and sees a labra-doodle dog approaching. She automatically interprets the situation as:

"Oh no! This monster is not on a leash! It will kill me!" Then she feels frightened.

This is the exact same situation being interpreted in four different ways and leading to four completely different emotional reactions. Given the specific interpretation of the situation, the emotional reactions make perfect sense for each individual. It would make no sense to feel panic in the presence of a dog that you interpreted as cute and friendly. Likewise, believing you are about to be mauled by a vicious German Shepherd and feeling joyful at the prospect seems a bit maladaptive.

The bottom line is that it is perfectly logical for you to feel afraid when a social (or other) situation is interpreted as threatening. The threat can be interpreted as immediate (the dog will bite or the plane will crash) or as something leading to long-term adverse consequences (I'll become an outcast of my community or I'll be unloved and die alone someday).

It is important for you to understand that these emotions you feel are based on your brain's *automatic* interpretations of a trigger. It is not your choice or fault—you have no control over the initial noise your brain makes in response to these triggers. Beating yourself up for a situation that is not your fault and that you have no control over (at least in the short term) will only serve to make you feel worse. We will talk about alternative ways to approach this brain noise a bit later.

Step 4: Avoidances and safety behaviors

Anxiety is an incredibly motivating emotion. When your brain thinks you are under threat, your body has an intense "fight-or-flight response," in which your heart rate rapidly escalates in order to pump more oxygen to your muscles to make them work quicker while adrenaline surges to give you an energy boost to make you run or fight more effectively. Fear is designed to quickly create a powerful bodily reaction so that you wake up and are laser-focused on your survival.

You wouldn't want to be relaxed and peaceful if you were being chased by a hungry bear—you'd get eaten! In the case of a phobia, your brain sees hungry bears where there aren't any. Your body's reaction, however, can be just as motivating—fight or run or die! It can be distracting at a party, to say the least.

It is not just people with phobias whose fight-or-flight alarm bells ring for misinterpretations. It happens to all of us on a regular basis.

- Your teenage daughter gets her license and drives off for the evening for the first time—and now she's thirty minutes past curfew and is not answering her cell phone.
- You are working peacefully in the garden in your yard—and a snake unexpectedly slithers by your foot (even a harmless one).
- You are giving a big presentation in class today—and are running twenty minutes late.
- You are at a crowded street festival enjoying the music—and you turn your head and suddenly can't spot your three-year-old.

So, what does your brain try to get you to do in the face a threat? It tries to get you to avoid the situation if possible. (If you see a bear, run the other way!) Or it uses safety behaviors to survive. (If you see a bear and can't run away, then grab a big stick and start swinging wildly while yodeling ferociously!) This is a great strategy if the danger is real, but not so helpful if the threat is only imagined.

Let's first look at direct avoidance.

When I got bit by the dog and was temporarily wary of dogs, I was directly exposed to dogs every day. If my parents had sensed my wariness and decided to overprotect me, they could have gotten rid of our dog. I could have stopped going over to friends' homes that had dogs. I could have avoided parks where dogs frequent, and TV shows and movies that have dogs in them. I could have left the room whenever someone even mentioned the "D-word." Those would have been examples of direct avoidances that would have grown my wariness into a phobia.

When it came to flying, however, I gave in to the temporary relief of avoidance. For ten years I avoided flying on small planes, flying at night, or sitting in the back of the plane (which I believed would be bumpier during turbulence). I turned down a number of events that I really would have liked to have attended because it would have meant another flight. I still flew once a year or so, but much less frequently out of irrational fear.

Avoidances are a significant factor in maintaining social phobias. You may avoid many or all of your triggers listed above, but you also might avoid things like eye contact, wearing certain types of clothing in social situations, and so on.

Brandon's Avoidances

- Parties
- Dating
- Public bathrooms
- Small talk
- Eye contact
- Self-disclosure
- Talking on the phone
- Raising my hand in class to ask a question
- Public speaking
- Crowds
- Playing on a sports team
- Asking a friend to hang out

EXERCISE: What types of situations or activities do you avoid because of your social fears?

....

....

....

....

....

....

....

....

....

....

....

....

....

....

....

....

....

....

....

....

....

....

....

Now let's look at safety behaviors.

When I first became concerned about flying (when thoughts of flying as being a life-threatening pursuit came across my radar), I promoted myself from airline passenger to airline backseat driver. I began to scan my environment on airplanes, looking for any signs of danger. When we hit turbulence, I would look out the window to check that we were not falling from the sky. I would tightly grip the armrests in either a desperate attempt to feel safer or perhaps as a primitive attempt to hold up the airplane. I would scan the facial expressions of the flight attendants to check to see whether they looked worried ... and so on!

Safety behaviors are things you do to feel safe when you can't directly avoid a phobic situation.

Here's what your anxiety doesn't want you to know ... safety behaviors don't really keep you safe!

Most people with a social phobia engage in many subtle and not-so-subtle safety behaviors when in uncomfortable social situations in order to ward off "catastrophic" rejection or humiliation.

Brandon's Safety Behaviors:

- ☒ Stare at cell phone rather than interact with others
- ☒ Only attend social event if you bring a friend or family member
- ☒ Stay in your head (internal focus) rather than in the moment (external focus)
- ☐ Prepare an excuse so you can be prepared to leave social event early
- ☐ Sit close to the exit or the end of a row in class—so you can flee whenever you want
- ☒ Wait until the last moment before deciding whether to attend social event
- ☐ Keep radio turned up in the car in order to avoid small talk or awkwardness
- ☐ Talk constantly to avoid awkward pauses or to prove you are smart
- ☒ Talk quietly to not draw attention
- ☒ Use your phone or other item to mentally escape from situation
- ☐ Look at floor
- ☒ Don't make eye contact
- ☒ Talk only to certain "comfortable" people

- ☒ Choose places least crowded
- ☒ Plan what you will say before speaking
- ☒ Review your social behavior "after-the-fact"—the "post mortem"
- ☒ Over-prepare for a social or performance event—five hours' prep for a two-minute talk
- ☐ Sit or stand away from others
- ☒ Tense up to feel more in control
- ☒ Rush through the social or performance event.
- ☒ Keep interactions as brief as possible
- ☒ Only socialize when feeling well rested, calm, having a good hair day, or whatever arbitrary rule anxiety imposes on you
- ☒ "Fight" to get rid of anxiety
- ☐ Try to block worried thoughts
- ☐ Drink alcohol at or before social event—because anxiety demands it!
- ☒ Keep earbuds in your ear so you don't have to interact with anyone
- ☐ Wear clothes that are not too attention getting—camouflage, anyone?
- ☐ Make an effort to fade into the background
- ☒ Keep conversation (or relationships) superficial
- ☒ Other: Avoid eating before socializing so bathroom breaks are less likely to be needed

EXERCISE: Check off your social anxiety safety behaviors

- ☐ Stare at cell phone rather than interact with others
- ☐ Only attend social event if you bring a friend or family member
- ☐ Stay in your head (internal focus) rather than in the moment (external focus)
- ☐ Prepare an excuse so you can be prepared to leave social event early
- ☐ Sit close to the exit or the end of a row in class—so you can flee whenever you want
- ☐ Wait until the last moment before deciding whether to attend social event

- ☐ Keep radio turned up in the car in order to avoid small talk or awkwardness
- ☐ Talk constantly to avoid awkward pauses or to prove you are smart
- ☐ Talk quietly to not draw attention
- ☐ Use your phone or other item to mentally escape from situation
- ☐ Look at floor
- ☐ Don't make eye contact
- ☐ Talk only to certain "comfortable" people
- ☐ Choose places least crowded
- ☐ Plan what you will say before speaking
- ☐ Review your social behavior "after-the-fact"—the "post mortem"
- ☐ Over-prepare for a social or performance event—five hours' prep for a two-minute talk
- ☐ Sit or stand away from others
- ☐ Tense up to feel more in control
- ☐ Rush through the social or performance event
- ☐ Keep interactions as brief as possible
- ☐ Only socialize when feeling well rested, calm, having a good hair day, or whatever arbitrary rule anxiety imposes on you
- ☐ "Fight" to get rid of anxiety
- ☐ Try to block worried thoughts
- ☐ Drink alcohol at or before social event—because anxiety demands it!
- ☐ Keep earbuds in your ear so you don't have to interact with anyone
- ☐ Wear clothes that are not too attention getting— camouflage, anyone?
- ☐ Make an effort to fade into the background
- ☐ Keep conversation (or relationships) superficial
- ☐ Other:
- ☐ Other:
- ☐ Other:

Step 5: Safety learning does NOT occur

When you have a fear of something that, inherently, is not dangerous, and you engage in avoidances and safety behaviors to prevent a catastrophic outcome, you do not get to learn that the situation was safe. Safety learning does not occur and therefore the fear remains or perhaps grows.

Here is my favorite vignette that highlights both the futility of avoidances and safety behaviors and their power to keep people stuck in a phobic cycle.

Suppose your friend Joey went with you to see a scary movie and afterwards became afraid that the Boogeyman was going to get him. You try to convince him that there really is no Boogeyman, but he isn't so easily convinced. He goes into full-Boogeyman prevention mode.

He begins to avoid:

* Going out after dark
* Saying the name "Boogeyman"
* Watching anything scary
* People wearing black clothing
* Anything Halloween-related

He begins to engage in **safety behaviors**:

* He bathes only in official church-sanctioned holy water
* He wears organic garlic cloves under his collar
* He checks the back seat of his car and under his bed daily for Boogeymen
* … and he calls you every day so you can reassure him that he did everything he could to ward off the Boogeyman

He does this for a few weeks and then when you meet up with him for coffee you ask Joey how his Boogeyman prevention strategies are working. He smiles excitedly and says, "It's working perfectly! I have not been attacked by any Boogeymen!"

Would he have been attacked by the Boogeyman had he not engaged in avoidances and safety behaviors? Of course not (with the possible exception of Los Angeles during a full moon!). However, because the dreaded attack did not happen in the face of these behaviors he *feels* like they are working … so he better keep them up or else! That is how phobias work, and social phobias are no exception.

Because his avoidances and safety behaviors *feel* necessary for keeping him safe, he is fooled into believing that they are preventing a calamity that is quite improbable.

Perfect Brandon

Brandon has a long history of social avoidance. When he does socialize, however, he attempts to project an unrealistic image of perfection, in both his appearance and his interpersonal style. As he goes through high school without experiencing the world-ending rejection that he worries about, he attributes this to a successful performance and feels he better keep it up or else! He doesn't dare let the world see the "real Brandon." The result, however, is that he does not get to learn that people would be okay with him simply being a regular imperfect (i.e., human) high school student. He feels his performance is "working" and therefore the show must go on or devastating rejection will be unleashed. He is trapped in the social phobia cycle!

As long as the danger interpretation remains the same, the anxiety remains the same

As long as you continue to truly believe that the plane will crash, the dog will kill, the Boogeyman will pounce, or that you will be rejected in a catastrophic way—the anxiety you experience is logical and it would not make sense to feel differently. For the anxiety to lessen, you need to learn that the catastrophic outcome will not occur—through facing your fears, repeatedly, without using avoidances or safety behaviors. If you spend ten hours with a dog that behaves in a friendly or neutral way and does not kill you, you will begin to learn that maybe dogs aren't so bad and that you can handle it—you will start to feel less frightened around them.

It is not enough, however, to just face your social fears—you must face them without engaging in your safety behaviors in order to see that the situation is inherently safe. We will discuss the specifics of these behavioral strategies later in the book.

On the surface, it sounds simple enough.

Anxiety, however, will not relinquish power over you so easily. It truly feels you are in danger, after all. It will use every trick in its rule book in order to keep you safe, even if that means you being stuck and afraid. That's the bad news.

The good news is ... you have access to anxiety's rule book!

If you can understand anxiety's rules, you can come up with counter-rules designed to help free you from the phobic cycle.

ANXIETY'S SECRET RULES

In order to "protect" you, I (Anxiety) am going to try to convince you that:

- *Scary thoughts should be taken seriously.*
- *It is extremely important (and possible) to get 100 percent certainty.*
- *Discomfort is bad and should be avoided.*
- *If something "feels" dangerous, then it probably is.*
- *Anxious thoughts and feelings should be fought off, hated, struggled against, and completely got rid of (and certainly never accepted).*
- *Fear is your fault!*

Follow these rules to stay stuck ... I mean safe.

Now, let's explore each of anxiety's rules and the counter-rules you can use to help escape from the phobic cycle.

Anxiety Rule 1: I will convince you that scary thoughts should be taken seriously.

Rejection, humiliation, degradation ... they're coming for you! Keep your guard up. Don't show any signs of weakness—they will pounce. You're not good enough. You're not smart enough. Don't even try. Leave before it is too late!

The brain is a noisy place. Most of the time, people are not paying attention to their thoughts, so the noise is resonating below the mental surface, in the unconscious. When you're in triggering situations, however, thoughts related to the frightening event become loud, urgent, and stuck on repeat.

Anxiety would like you to believe that these thoughts are facts. Imagine you are giving a presentation at a meeting and the thought pops into your head that, "No one here likes you and you should shut up now!" Anxiety would then like you to *behave* as if that thought were a fact and engage in avoidances and safety behaviors. The interesting thing is that no matter how much anxiety shouts, "You are being rejected!", it in no way changes external reality and has NO control over your behaviors unless you give it power by acting as if the thought were true.

Our brains are non-stop noise machines. Thoughts jabber on all day and even while we sleep. This is not psychopathology, but simply the background music to our lives. The content of your thoughts certainly is shaped by experiences, but all brains are noisy places and unpleasant thoughts reside within the constant stream of everyone's thoughts, same as with pleasant and neutral thoughts.

Think about your brain noise as being similar to the results of an internet search. Take the book you are holding, for example. If you type the word "book" into an internet search engine, you will bring up thousands of "hits." Some of these will be pleasant, such as books that you are interested in reading. Others will be books that are neutral for many of us, such as how to rebuild broken appliances. There will be other hits, however, that will be very dark and disturbing, which run counter to your values or desires. You have no control over the results of your internet search and are therefore not responsible for that outcome, nor do you have to take action based on what presents itself.

Just like the hits you get from that internet search, thoughts of all kinds automatically pop up. We will spend a lot of time in this book discussing what to do with them, but what is important for you to understand at this point is that acting as if these anxiety-thoughts are vitally important information is bound to lead to avoidances and safety behaviors, which as you know, will then maintain or worsen the impact of social anxiety on your life.

So, for now, when anxiety presents you with scary thoughts, simply accept them as thoughts rather than facts. For example, if you are about to give a presentation at work and anxiety says, "You will screw up and get fired!", rather than falling back on avoidances and safety behaviors, simply acknowledge that you are aware that you are having the thought that you will screw up and get fired. You are not your thoughts and thoughts are not facts! You are the observer of your thoughts and you alone have the power to act on them OR choose not act on them.

You do not, however, have the power to get rid of your automatic thoughts through sheer force of will. Have you ever had a song stuck in your head? What happened why you tried to force it away? Right! It only got louder and stickier.

TRY AN EXPERIMENT: Enter a mild to moderately uncomfortable social situation. Observe your thoughts and simply acknowledge them by labeling them as "thoughts." Practice accepting these thoughts as normal brain noise and let them play in the background while you go about your business.

Brandon

I chose to go to the farmer's market with my parents last Thursday. Normally I tell them that I don't want to come because it's "boring." The reality is that the large crowd makes me very uncomfortable. I went and let the noise be the noise—and you know what? It didn't bother me as much!

EXERCISE: Now it's your turn.

For my experiment I chose:

....

....

What was it like for you to begin to view your automatic thoughts as brain noise rather than absolute facts?

....

....

....

....

....

....

....

....

....

....

You will learn a lot more about coping and thriving with anxiety thoughts later in the book.

Anxiety Rule 2: I will convince you that it is extremely important (and possible) to get 100 percent certainty.

When I used to feel panicked on airplanes, ultimately what I wanted was to be 100 percent certain that the plane was not going to crash. Your social anxiety leads you to wanting 100 percent certainty that the person you ask on a date will say "yes," that your speech will be well received by everybody who hears it, and that no one will mind in the least if you make a social mistake.

Wouldn't 100 percent certainty be a great thing? I agree, however, it will never happen. Life is uncertain.

Anxiety always wants us to achieve the mythic 100 percent certainty, but there are two main problems with this:

1. It will never happen.
2. The more you avoid embracing uncertainty, the more your ability to tolerate normal life uncertainty diminishes.

The reality is that life IS uncertain—therefore, building up your ability to tolerate uncertainty seems to be an adaptive life skill.

Anxiety wants you to desperately try to achieve 100 percent certainty, therefore your counter-rule is to seek out and embrace uncertainty as a way to build up your uncertainty-tolerance muscles. You benefit when you go toward what anxiety tells you to stay away from. When those feelings of uncertainty spring up, you can remind yourself that this is your uncertainty-tolerance workout for the day and open up to it rather than fighting for certainty. Let go and embrace not knowing for sure.

Try to get an uncertainty-tolerance workout as often as you can.

CHALLENGE YOURSELF WITH THE FOLLOWING EXPERIMENT: Enter a social situation that is mildly to moderately social anxiety triggering. Notice those feelings of uncertainty: *What are they thinking about me? Am I behaving okay? Do I belong here?* Instead of labeling them as something that needs fixing, allow them to remain. Be willing to temporarily accept and embrace that uncertainty and label it as a desirable workout goal.

EXERCISE: What did you do and how did it go? How was that different from fighting for certainty?

....

....

....

....

....

....

Anxiety Rule 3: I will convince you that discomfort is bad and should be avoided.

Very often people are waiting for the magical day when all social discomfort has vanished in order to face their social fears. However, we know that people need to repeatedly face their social fears (without safety behaviors) in order to learn that they are not at great risk for catastrophe. Only then will they begin to feel less uncomfortable in those situations. If someone is frightened of public speaking, they begin to feel better only after having spent a significant amount of time speaking publically while observing that nothing terrible has happened. Waiting to feel better before facing your social fears is backward and ineffective. You could wait the rest of your life.

Discomfort in life (social and otherwise) is normal and unavoidable. Similar to uncertainty, if you run away from social discomfort, your ability to tolerate future discomfort shrinks. You can build up your social discomfort tolerance muscles by fostering a willingness to open up to the discomfort rather than making anxious discomfort your enemy. If you are like most people, you will experience emotional discomfort throughout life (even on the very best of days, there will be at least trace amounts). You can suffer less and make progress on your social and life goals by changing your relationship with discomfort rather than seek the impossible by working to avoid it altogether. Fostering a willing experience of discomfort strengthens your ability to cope with the challenges that life will throw at you.

Think about how many social opportunities you have turned down because you felt it would be uncomfortable to attend. Instead, what if you built up your anxiety tolerance by entering socially uncomfortable situations just *because* they are uncomfortable? Then, practice willingness to coexist with the discomfort, softening into it and embracing it, acknowledging it without condemning it as "bad or wrong."

EXERCISE: Enter a social situation that is mildly to moderately anxiety provoking. Notice those feelings of discomfort that emerge with the anxiety. Instead of labeling them as "bad" and resisting them, tell yourself that you are choosing to have your discomfort-tolerance workout for the day. ("No pain, no gain!") Soften into your experience of the discomfort rather than tightening up to try to force it away.

What did you do and how did it go? How was this experience different from labeling the discomfort as something that MUST go away and fighting to get rid of it?

....

....

....

....

....

....

....

Anxiety Rule 4: I will convince you that if something feels dangerous, then it is dangerous.

This is known as "Emotional Reasoning." Why did I worry that the plane I was in was going to fall out of the sky? When turbulence struck, it really felt to me like the plane was going down!

Emotional reasoning occurs when the primary evidence you have for why the anxious thought is true is that you feel frightened by it. It is your gut instinct gone awry.

Florence

Florence's big moment was coming up. She'd been a member of her church choir for the past thirty years and now the new director had given her a solo. This was to be her moment in the spotlight. As she stood trembling amongst the other singers, her heart was pounding and she felt herself beginning to blush. Anxiety was screaming at her, "You're going to mess this up! Why did you agree to this? You are about to be utterly humiliated!" She experienced a flood of panic and despair. She knew this was going to be disastrous.

Since all phobias involve reasonably safe situations being misinterpreted as dangerous, emotional reasoning typically plays a big role.

- The elevator will get stuck and I will suffocate.
- Snakes will find me and get me.
- The Boogeyman is out there.
- I will be the laughing stock of the entire college if I spill my drink at the party.

These thoughts may at times feel very convincing even when there is no evidence of their accuracy other than the feelings of danger themselves. (*I feel in danger, therefore I am in danger.*)

So, how reliable is emotional reasoning? Think about it this way: You are watching the trial of an accused murderer and the prosecutor presents her evidence of guilt like this:

> *"Your honor, the defendant, Colonel Mustard, is clearly guilty of killing Miss Scarlet in the observatory with the candlestick because he just kinda freaks me out!"*

What would you think about that evidence if you were on the jury? What would the judge's likely reaction be?

> *"Is that all you've got? Well then, case dismissed!"*

If the reasoning behind your social fears is similar to this, do you want to continue to let this emotional "evidence" control your movement (or lack of movement) toward your social goals?

If not, try acknowledging that your body is likely overreacting. Continue to behave as if the situation were safe even though it feels otherwise. Don't fall for the emotional reasoning trap. When hit with the fear, accept the initial bodily response and continue to move forward toward your social goals.

REMEMBER: Feelings are not facts.

EXERCISE: List the situations in your life where emotional reasoning has led you to draw conclusions based on little to no actual evidence. Are you willing to learn how to move forward with your social goals despite your initial anxiety-driven reaction?

....

....

....

....

....

....

....

....

....

....

....

Anxiety Rule 5: I will convince you that anxious thoughts and feelings should be fought off, hated, struggled against, and completely got rid of (and certainly never accepted).

Samuel

After his marriage of fifteen years ended, Samuel worried he would never find love again. Yet, his friends convinced him to try internet dating and here he was at an Italian restaurant sharing breadsticks with Shoshana. "Just relax and be yourself," his friends had advised. But he was trying fricking hard to relax and it was not fricking working! He was so worried that his anxiety was going to draw unwanted attention that he tightened his muscles to try to keep from shaking, but that only made him feel worse—and snap off half his breadstick, which flew onto the adjacent table, startling a four-year-old whose parents were lost in conversation. He quickly excused himself and casually fled to the restroom. There, he sat desperately in his stall, door locked, and impulsively downloaded a relaxation app on his phone. His struggle to achieve a Zen state only served to further ramp up his anxiety. *What will Shoshana think?*

Social anxiety dangles this rule in front of us and it is so tempting to latch on. When people feel uncomfortable in social situations, it is normal to wish that the scary thoughts and feelings go away. It is also normal to fight these thoughts and feelings, tighten against them, and struggle to get rid of them.

It is the paradox of anxiety that when you don't want it, you've got more of it. When you fight it, it gets stronger and your sense of suffering increases. On the other hand, it is possible to accept that, at this point in time (at the party, on a date, or giving a speech), your mind is generating thoughts that are triggering your fight-or-flight response and leading your body to produce unpleasant sensations. When you can let go of fighting these thoughts and sensations, and allow them to run their course without resistance, you will likely suffer less.

EXERCISE PART A: Enter a social situation that normally leads to increased anxiety. Don't do anything different than you would normally do. This is only a fact-finding mission. Simply notice your natural tendency to struggle against what you are experiencing. Observe where you tighten your body the most. Are you tensing the muscles in your chest, shoulders, jaw, hands, stomach, arms, legs, or other body part? On a scale from zero to ten, notice how much you struggle in these areas. A ten means you are struggling with everything you've got! Also, notice whether you tend to hold your breath or breathe shallowly. This is another sure sign of struggle.

Where in your body did you notice the struggle occurring? Did you hold your breath or breathe shallowly?

....

....

....

The struggle can also be mental:

* I hate this!
* I've got to get rid of these anxious thoughts.
* I must distract myself.

In what ways did you notice a mental struggle?

....

....

....

....

....

....

....

....

....

....

....

EXERCISE PART B: Once you've completed Part A, let's continue the experiment a different way.

Enter another social situation that elicits very similar amounts of anxiety. This time, however, do not struggle against the anxiety. Let go, temporarily, of trying to make yourself feel better. Instead of tightening up against anxiety, *invite it to be there with your permission.* Soften into the experience and give anxiety permission to be background noise for the moment. Let go of your resistance and simply allow it to run its course naturally—neither pull it close to over-examine it nor push it away to get rid of it. Just simply and softly coexist.

Also let go of the mental struggle. Let anxiety shout boisterously in the background, *"Failure, rejection, and catastrophe!"* Passively acknowledge the "noise" and let go of the urge to take the bait and mentally fight back. For now, just allow it be background noise.

Now, how was your experience during Part B different from your experience in Part A? Did you suffer more when trying to fight off the anxiety or when you opened up to it?

....

....

....

....

....

....

....

The Nightmare

Tom comes home after a long day at work. He enters the house, shuts the door, and is whacked in the head by a baseball bat. He is knocked unconscious. He awakens to find himself strapped to a chair. Around his arm is a monitor that projects his heart rate onto the computer screen in front of him. Three unsavory young men stand around him. They all have guns pointed at him and look to be having sadistic fun. The leader leans in close and explains, "It's very simple— relax or die!"

Could you relax? What happens when anxiety commands you to "relax or else"?

Anxiety Rule 6: I will convince you that fear is your fault!

What Shoshana Thought

"What a total loser I am!" Shoshana thought as her date Samuel abruptly left her alone at the table. "Here I am, a supposedly confident middle-aged woman and I am still feeling so shy and uncomfortable just having a dinner date!"

And there she sat, buying into the thoughts that she was weak and worthless because of the way she felt—her blind-date jitters were quickly evolving into sadness and self-loathing.

Anxiety can be downright mean! Sometimes as a last-ditch attempt to keep you stuck in a socially avoidant cycle, anxiety may try to demoralize you. It does this by calling you names ...

- Weak!
- Inept!
- Failure!

... and so forth, and trying to convince you that the anxiety you feel is all your fault and if you weren't such a [fill in your duly designated epithet], then you would feel calm and socially confident in those triggering situations.

If you fall for this and jump on the "beat up on me bandwagon," your energy and will to courageously face your social fears becomes diminished. The siren call to avoidance then grows louder and more persuasive. Anxiety does not do this because it is trying to hurt you; it just wants you to maintain the avoidant status quo.

So, what can you do to counter the blame and shame that anxiety throws at you?

There is an emerging trend in the field of mental health that is really catching on (though Buddhists have been practicing it for 2,500 years). It involves fostering compassion for oneself and others as a pathway to a more satisfying (and less demoralizing) life. Nowhere do I see the necessity of fostering compassion as more important than with social anxiety.

As we have discussed, social anxiety is normal. Even phobic social anxiety often builds in slow, subtle, and sneaky ways. Whatever the reasons that you may have gotten stuck in a socially phobic cycle, it is now yours to do with what you will. You own it, despite the fact that you did not wish to buy it. Showing compassion for yourself can make the progress of getting unstuck and moving forward less painful.

LET'S TRY AN EXPERIMENT:

PART A: Enter a social situation that is uncomfortable. Notice the self-condemnations that are automatically present in your mind. List them below:

....

....

....

....

....

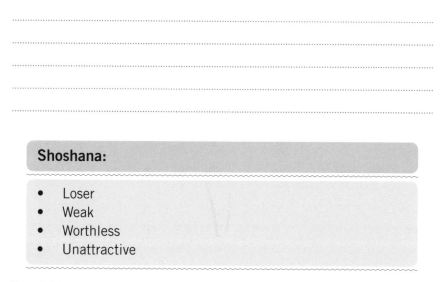

Shoshana:

- Loser
- Weak
- Worthless
- Unattractive

In addition to the anxiety that is present, what other feelings come up with the self-condemnations?

....

....

....

....

....

Shoshana:

- Frustration
- Sadness
- Self-loathing

PART B: Now enter another uncomfortable situation. This time, try bringing with you the notion that the anxiety you feel is not your fault and that you are absolutely an okay person no matter what types of mental noise and emotions you experience. Try to accept and embrace the notion that: "It is okay that I am experiencing .... (see part A)."

How was this different?

....

....

....

....

....

....

....

Can you begin to direct a bit more compassion your way when social anxiety tries to demoralize you? Can you embrace the wisdom of no-blame?

Imagine that you woke up this morning with a case of the flu. If you've ever had the flu before, you know how uncomfortable it can be. Like most people, you probably would be disappointed that you have the flu and might need some last-minute scrambling to arrange for your absence from school or work that day. Then, you'd likely relax the best way you could. Yes, it's a bummer to have the flu, but you may choose to warm up some soup, lie down, relax, and catch a movie on TV. You'd take care of yourself.

Hopefully, you would not call yourself a worthless loser for having a nasty viral infection. You'd likely cut yourself some slack. Why take such a different approach for coping with the reality of social discomfort that is equally not your fault and may be just as uncomfortable?

SOCIAL ANXIETY'S RULES TO KEEP YOU STUCK—BOTTOM LINE

Believe it or not, your anxiety is designed to help you. If you were truly in danger, wouldn't you want an ally who would do whatever it takes to keep you safe? Anxiety's rules are designed to keep you safe from the dangers of other people. The problem is when these rules persuade you to stay away from those social encounters that would help you break out of a social phobic cycle and serve to further your social goals.

My Counter-Rules for Coping and Thriving with Social Anxiety

Anxiety Says:	I'll Choose To:
Take your thoughts very seriously!	Accept all thoughts—they're just thoughts. Fighting them only makes anxiety worse.
You must be 100 percent certain.	Nothing is 100 percent certain. Trying to be certain only makes anxiety worse. Instead, I will seek out and accept uncertainty.
Discomfort is bad.	Discomfort is only discomfort. Fighting discomfort only makes anxiety worse. I will seek out and accept discomfort.
If something feels dangerous, then it is dangerous.	I won't fall for that trick. How many times have my worst fears come true? I can accept these feelings and go toward my social goals.
You'd better get rid of me 100 percent.	I can let anxiety be background noise.
Fear is your fault!	I didn't choose my upbringing or physiology. This is not my fault, but I can take steps to move toward my social goals.

PHOBIC SOCIAL ANXIETY SUMMARY

Social discomfort is a normal human experience, even on a daily basis to some degree. Rather than heaping shame upon yourself for these unavoidable thoughts and feelings, you can choose to foster an acceptance of them as a natural part of life and learn to cope and even thrive in their presence.

Social anxiety, however, can turn phobic in one or more areas when it convinces you to latch onto your scary thoughts about interpersonal or performance situations and then treat these thoughts as if they were facts. This leads you to try to escape perceived social "danger" through a regular pattern of avoidances and safety behaviors.

This creates a maladaptive cycle with social danger thoughts leading to increased anxiety, which then leads to avoidances and safety behaviors, which leads to more danger thoughts, and so on.

It's time to learn more about how to break this cycle!

Introduction to Cognitive Behavioral Therapy 2.0

How ancient wisdom with a modern approach can benefit you

Sarah

After six painful months of unemployment, Sarah had been offered and accepted the job of her dreams—human resources director of a flourishing tech start-up. She made sure to be one of the first to show up for work in the morning and one of the last to leave in the evening. In her new job role, she "appeared" to be comfortable interacting with her boss and coworkers. She took great pains to present herself as confident, poised, and in her element at all times.

On the inside, however, she lived in constant fear of people seeing behind her "act." If she let her guard down for a moment, she was sure that she'd be discovered to be the fraud she felt herself to be. If they only knew the real her, it would all come crumbling down—at least that's what her anxiety told her.

So, she went on living and hiding behind her façade. Socializing became an exhausting performance. She went on a few dates, but always broke things off after just a couple of weeks out of fear that her potential romantic partner would accidently see the "real" her. And she absolutely would not allow that to happen!

TO CBT AND BEYOND!

Bottom line: You'd like to go after your social goals without social anxiety blocking you or making you suffer miserably along the way. You've now armed yourself with an understanding of what makes your social anxiety tick. Now it's time to move forward toward your social courage goals using state-of-the-art psychological strategies.

Cognitive Behavioral Therapy (CBT) is a scientifically proven set of mental-health-promoting strategies that deal with unhelpful thoughts (cognitive) and behaviors and how they impact your emotions (or how your emotions impact your thoughts and behaviors). The goal of traditional CBT for social anxiety is to decrease social anxiety by doing something differently with your thoughts and behaviors. CBT's primary focus is on symptom reduction or elimination.

As discussed earlier, however, social anxiety is normal, so elimination is not an option. And, while symptom reduction can and does occur, you still need strategies to cope and thrive with residual social anxiety. That is where newer approaches (based on far older Eastern philosophies) come in.

Rather than limiting yourself to old-school CBT, the rest of the book focuses on a more modern take on CBT—one that is infused with ancient wisdom (mindfulness, acceptance, and compassion) to create what I playfully call CBT 2.0.

CBT 2.0 integrates newer strategies within a comprehensive modern CBT approach. These strategies are called "third wave" to represent a shift over time in what some people consider to be an improvement to traditional CBT. The first wave involved a singular focus on altering behaviors to decrease psychological symptoms. The second wave (which was added to the strategies of the first) involved changing irrational thoughts to decrease psychological symptoms. The third-wave approach involves changing how you interact with your thoughts and emotions rather than altering them directly in any way.

Both traditional CBT and third-wave strategies can be used to help you lessen control that social anxiety has over you. Both approaches are backed up by significant amounts of scientific research, attesting to their efficacy.

Surfing the third wave

If you have an unpleasant thought ("People don't like me"), traditional CBT would encourage you to change that thought into a new, more adaptive thought. In this model, the thought is the problem and changing the thought is the solution. ("Actually, there is evidence that some people do like me.")

The problem with changing this thought is that even when you no longer believe the thought, the little imp in your brain, your anxiety, may keep yelling the thought at you. You can end up in an endless mental tug-of-war game of "yes, they do like me … no, they don't like you … yes, they do like me … " That is certainly not a fun or productive way to spend a Saturday night!

Third-wave approaches (such as Acceptance and Commitment Therapy and Compassion-Focused Therapy) suggest that it is futile to try to change thoughts. Trying to change them just makes you roll around in the verbal muck in your brain to no positive end. Rather than trying to change your thoughts themselves, these approaches encourage you to change your relationship with these thoughts ("I am aware of the thought that nobody likes me … it's okay for me to coexist with that thought") while moving toward valued goals—all while being nice to yourself rather than condemning yourself for your experience. We will go into more detail on third-wave approaches in the next few chapters.

CBT 2.0: Merging two great approaches

Unfortunately, gurus of CBT and third-wave strategies often battle it out (i.e., debate amicably at conferences and hotel bar happy hours) over which strategy is the "right" one. Proponents of the third-wave approaches often seek to toss out traditional CBT altogether.

CBT 2.0 takes the best of both the traditional CBT approach and the third-wave approaches and integrates them into a comprehensive approach for dealing with challenging thoughts, feelings, and behaviors.

Why must you choose from macaroni or cheese, peanut butter or jelly, or traditional CBT or third-wave approaches when they go so well together?

OVERVIEW OF USING CBT 2.0 TO COPE AND THRIVE WITH SOCIAL ANXIETY

As long as you get hooked by your automatic socially anxious thoughts or beliefs and flee from the ensuing emotional discomfort by avoiding uncomfortable situations or relying on safety behaviors, you feed the social anxiety, making it stronger and louder.

The CBT 2.0 approach to coping and thriving with social anxiety aims to unhook you from these thoughts and encourage you to face your social fears while coping effectively with uncomfortable emotions. The upcoming chapters aims to help you to achieve the following:

1. Acknowledge without condemning the scary thoughts your brain is producing.
2. Cope with your thoughts through mindful acceptance and defusion while gently, compassionately, and logically challenging unhelpful beliefs.
3. Utilize a variety of strategies for coping with your anxious discomfort while building up your anxiety-tolerance muscles.

4. Repeatedly move toward triggering social situations (with open eyes and an open mind) in order to learn that the situation is not truly dangerous, build up your anxiety tolerance muscles, and progress toward your social goals.
5. Solve challenges that come up along the way.

You've now learned a lot about your social anxiety and have had an overview of the CBT 2.0 approach. Now it's time for the fun to begin. Now it is time to actively move forward.

4

Brain Noise

Core skills for coping with socially anxious thoughts and beliefs

---

Cassie

Cassie, the only child of a single mother, had never spent much time around boys. She attended a prestigious all-girls Catholic school and had been painfully shy interacting with her male teachers. Now she was a freshman at a large university and the topic of guys and dating was frequently the source of conversation among her new friends. Not only had she never dated, boys were very scary to even speak to! She could not imagine one ever showing an interest in her. Why would they? But if they did ... that was a much more terrifying thought! Either she would spend her life alone or would have to face the terror of dating. She was sure that she was destined to be alone forever.

INTRODUCTION

As we've discussed, our brains are noisy "better-safe-than-sorry" devices. There is no existing therapy that will change the regular presence of anxiety thoughts. You have no choice as to whether those thoughts are going to occur in a given situation. They are automatic. The goal, therefore, is not to make them stop, but to react adaptively when they arise.

So, what should you do with thoughts that pop into your mind and lead you to feeling frightened and/or demoralized? Thoughts such as:

- No one here likes you.
- You shouldn't be such an awkward loser.
- You're screwing this up!
- People think you are anxious and pathetic.
- You are absolutely unlovable.
- They're going to laugh at you if you talk to them.

The core skills for dealing with these social anxiety thoughts that are discussed in this section include:

- Logical and Compassionate Reframes
- Mindful Acceptance
- Defusion

These skills have a significant amount of scientific research demonstrating their usefulness. Which of these skills or combination of skills you use will vary based on the situation.

Here's the bottom line. When you enter certain social situations, your brain produces scary thoughts that then lead you to feel frightened. Or, you may avoid these situations altogether because these thoughts were intimidating or demoralizing.

You have four options for dealing with these thoughts.

1. Agree with the thoughts and behave as if they were true. This is probably what you have been doing at least some of the time. The advantage of this approach is that you don't have to do anything different and can stick to the status quo without making the effort to change. The disadvantage is that anxiety retains more control over your life than you'd like.

2. You can try to use avoidant strategies such as fighting the thoughts, distracting yourself, or using substances to numb out. For some, it may even "help" in the short term, but over the long run,

avoidant strategies allow these thoughts to maintain their grip on you—and you may wind up with a serious addiction that certainly can be an obstacle to getting your social needs met.

3. You can put them under the microscope—logically examining the evidence for and against the content of your thoughts. If they fail the logic test, you can come up with a more adaptive thought. This is known as "cognitive therapy."

4. You can mindfully accept their presence, see them simply as brain noises, and work to accept the presence of the noise while defusing from the content of the thoughts. "Defusing" means becoming less attached to the thought—so that it is just noise rather than a command that needs to be acted on.

If you want to cope and thrive with social anxiety, you can rule out options one and two. As you have learned, these strategies lead to avoidances or safety behaviors, which in the long run, maintain or exacerbate social anxiety's control over you.

This leads you to options three or four. Do you pick apart the content of these thoughts OR do you accept the process of brain noise and detach from the thoughts?

THE GURUS' DISAGREEMENT

The gurus of cognitive therapy will recommend picking the thoughts apart and using logic to change the old thoughts into more adaptive new ones. Not so fast, the gurus of mindfulness and acceptance-based strategies will caution you. They will tell you that you should never sink to the level of dealing with the content of anxiety-thoughts—that you should not dignify the thoughts by directly engaging with them.

Does it really have to be either—or?

One of the great advantages of not being a guru is that I am not locked into a particular mindset. I find great value in *both* of these strategies and think that each can be used in a way that is tremendously helpful. At the risk of upsetting the gurus who fall into the "it's my way or the highway" camp, you can integrate both of these approaches into a strategy for dealing with social anxiety thoughts.

To put it concisely, when anxiety gives you a scary thought that you truly believe, then start with examining the logic behind it. However, once you realize that the noise in your mind is illogical and you no longer believe it (even though it may *feel* real at times)—then practice acceptance and detachment strategies and move forward with your social goals.

My Flying Phobia

When I was terrified to fly, anxiety would shout in my ear, "This is incredibly dangerous!" and "We're going to crash!" with every turbulent bump. My belief at that time was that a multi-ton metal vehicle hurling through the atmosphere at thirty thousand feet, held up merely by air, was an incredibly dangerous and foolhardy form of transportation. The logic center of my brain really believed it was dangerous. I needed to put my belief under the microscope, learn some facts, and then my belief changed to, "Even though flying feels to me to be incredibly dangerous, it is without a doubt the safest way to travel."

Once I realized that flying was safe, I was able to practice accepting and defusing from the thought that I was in danger when it popped up during turbulent flights. I no longer believed flying was dangerous, even though I still have that thought as background noise periodically.

Next, we'll look at common types of social anxiety thoughts.

> *"Nobody likes me. Everybody hates me. Guess I'll go eat worms."*
> Either lyrics from a "delightful" American nursery rhyme or
> the social anxiety national anthem

COMMON TYPES OF SOCIAL ANXIETY THOUGHTS

In the previous section on understanding social anxiety, you learned about social anxiety's rules that were designed to keep you from facing your social fears. These rules seem to impact most people who are struggling with phobic social anxiety.

The following are types of social anxiety thoughts that may get triggered before, during, or after social situations. Most of us fall for some of these every now and again. You will likely relate to some or most, but not necessarily all of them.

Dr. Aaron Beck, the father of cognitive therapy, describes these types of thoughts as "cognitive distortions," which means they are errors that brains make at times. They relate to how you process certain information about yourself, the world (and people) around you, or your future. Again, it is normal for brains to generate these thoughts (or errors) at times, though when you find that they cause you to suffer or miss out on social opportunities, they become a problem.

Let's now take a look at each of these cognitive distortions. If you notice that there might be some overlap between them, you would be perceptive and correct.

Mind Reading
Description: Thoughts pertaining to what other people are thinking about you or feeling toward you.

Examples:

- "No one here likes me."
- "She thinks I'm boring."
- "He thinks I'm too awkward."

Fortune Telling
Description: Negative predictive thoughts about your future.

Examples:

- "No one will like me at the party."

- "My speech is going to bomb."
- "No one will ever want to date me."

Catastrophizing

Description: Thoughts that things in your life will be absolutely unbearable and you will be unable to cope. Whereas fortune-telling thoughts pertain to future rejections or failures, catastrophizing thoughts emphasize that these events will be utterly cataclysmic!

Examples:

- "If I get rejected, I'll be utterly destroyed."
- "If I make a mistake during my speech, I'll be the laughing stock of the entire school."
- "If I fail, my life will be ruined and I'll never get over it."

Labeling

Description: These thoughts shove the wonderfully complex you into a globally negative category. In other words, anxiety calls you names.

Examples:

- "Because I spilled my drink, I am a loser."
- "Because she turned me down for a date, I am completely unlovable."
- "Because I gave the wrong answer, I am stupid."

Discounting the Positives

Description: These thoughts minimize or discount the positive actions you take or good experiences you have with other people. The theme may be that when good things happen to you it is because of luck or pity.

Examples:

- "She only complimented me because she feels sorry for me."
- "He agreed to meet me for coffee because he feels obligated."
- "I only did well on the test because I got lucky."

Negative Filter

Description: These thoughts arise from selective attention to negative incidences while not taking in positive experiences with others.

Examples:

- "That didn't go well"—when returning home from a party where you had five pleasant conversations and a tasty dinner, but what is recalled is when a sixth person abruptly ended your conversation.
- "I'm a boring speaker"—when giving a speech and noticing one person playing on their cell phone, but not paying attention to the twenty people who appeared engaged and interested.

Overgeneralizing

Description: Thinking that isolated incidents are a continuous occurrence.

Examples:

- Your mind goes blank when asked a question— "This ALWAYS happens to me."
- You spill a drink at a party—"I do this EVERY time."
- You call someone by the wrong name—"I can never remember people's names."

All-or-Nothing Thinking

Description: Also known as "black-or-white" or "dichotomous" thinking, it involves thinking in extremes of "It is either all good or all bad", with no gray area or wiggle room in the middle.

Examples:

- "I'm either the life of the party or I'm a complete dud."
- "I'm either suave like James Bond or I'm completely socially inept."
- "If my appearance isn't flawless, then I am hideous."

Shoulds

Description: Psychology guru Albert Ellis described having these thoughts as "shoulding on yourself." Rather than thinking about how you might prefer things in life to be, you have thoughts that things should, must, or ought to be the way you want them to be.

Examples:

- "Everyone should like me."
- "I must present myself as witty and outgoing at all times."
- "My appearance has to be flawless."
- "I must never let people see me make a mistake!"

Personalizing

Description: These thoughts tell you that if something goes wrong socially, it is all your fault and your responsibility to fix it—rather than it being shared responsibility or someone else's responsibility altogether.

Examples:

- There's an awkward pause in a conversation—
  "I'm really blowing it."
- A person in the audience looks bored—"I must be a boring speaker."
- Your friend cancels plans for this evening—"I must be doing something wrong."

Unfair Comparisons

Description: These are thoughts that compare you to an extreme and then when you don't match up, there are thoughts that you aren't good enough.

Examples:

- "I must be as smart as the smartest person in my class."
- "I must be as witty as the guy at work who is always the life of the party."
- "I must be as attractive as that heavily Photoshopped supermodel—or life just stinks."

Wishing Ritual

Description: These thoughts focus on wishing something about you or your life was different, rather than making the best of how things are in reality.

Examples.

"If only I was ...
* taller
* shorter
* thinner
* bigger
* not bald
* not so hairy
* smarter
* funnier
* more serious
* more suave
* less awkward

... then I would go out and pursue my social goals!"

Perfectionism

Description: Thoughts that you and/or other people must be perfect— nothing short of perfection is acceptable.

Examples:

(Self)
* "I need to look and act perfectly at all times."
(Others)
* "My friend Susie was five minutes late. She does not respect my time—bad Susie!"

EXERCISE: Place a checkmark next to the type of thoughts you notice on a regular basis:

	Mind Reading
	Fortune Telling
	Catastrophizing
	Labeling
	Discounting the Positives
	Negative Filter
	Overgeneralizing
	All-or-Nothing Thinking
	Shoulds
	Personalizing
	Unfair Comparisons
	Wishing Ritual
	Perfectionism

Ask yourself:

"Do these thoughts cause me a lot of distress or do they interfere with progressing toward my social goals?"

The next questions to ask yourself are:

"Do I tend to believe these thoughts? Do they seem true?"

If the answer is "yes," then they are beliefs. In the next section you will learn how to apply the tools of logic and compassion in order to see things from a more adaptive point of view. Sometimes I think of this process of loosening up rigid beliefs as mental yoga—you are going to learn to be more flexible rather than tightly clenching around your unhelpful beliefs.

Once these thoughts are no longer beliefs that hold you back, then you will learn ways to recognize these thoughts simply as noise of the mind that no longer needs to control your destiny.

LOGICAL CHALLENGES TO ANXIETY THOUGHTS

"Men are disturbed not by the things that happen, but by their opinion of the things that happen."

Epictetus

Logical arguments are those that would stand up in a court of law when presented to an unbiased judge. Take the concept of airline safety. Use of observable, measurable data, such as the vast number of successful flights relative to the miniscule number of flying fatalities would be considered good evidence that flying is safe. On the contrary, "Flying is dangerous because it feels scary" would be poor evidence.

> *Anxiety Thought: My plane is going to crash!*
> *Logical Thought: Flying is the safest form of transportation. Feeling frightened does not change that fact.*

Are you wondering, *Isn't this the same as positive thinking?*

No. Logical thinking attempts to look at the situation just as it is. Your social anxiety thought may be true. If your thought is that you would be rejected as a candidate for president of the United States (or Queen of England), you would not be best served by telling yourself, "Just buck up, you'll be president or queen someday if you just work hard enough." In this case a logical thought might be, "It is okay not to be president or queen. Most people are neither and manage to get by somehow."

I once heard it said that a positive thinker sees the glass as half full while a negative thinker sees the glass as half empty. The logical thinker simply sees an eight-ounce glass containing four ounces of fluid.

Now let's look at more logical responses to common social anxiety thoughts.

Mind Reading

What anxiety doesn't want you to know is that unless you have superpowers and are regularly featured in movies and comic books, then you can't actually know what another person is thinking! Sure, you could ask them what they were thinking about, but (a) they may not tell you the truth, or (b) they may not have been paying attention to what they were thinking. They may not even have been thinking about you. They may have been thinking about their headache, unpaid bills, or their great Aunt Nona's delicious sweet potato pie.

Since you can't read minds, the best you can do is observe other people's behavior. If you ask someone on a date and they say "No thanks," there is a good chance that they are thinking that they do not wish to go on a date with you at this time. Non-verbally, you might notice that the person avoids making eye contact and ends the conversation quickly. Again, it would be reasonable to draw the conclusion that they are not interested based on those data points.

However, someone might say "No thanks" to a date because they have a prior commitment or are in a relationship already, but still find you attractive and would have said "yes" had the circumstances been different. They may avoid eye contact and end the conversation quickly due to their own anxiety or acute flatulence rather than them not finding you attractive.

As you can see, interpreting other people's behaviors can be challenging, but it is the best you have since you cannot read minds. Sometimes behavior interpretation is much easier. For example, if you ask that person on a date and they give you a big smile with prolonged eye contact, then give you a hug and state, "I was hoping you'd ask because I have had a huge crush on you since the third grade!", then guessing what they are thinking about you may not seem so difficult.

When you catch yourself believing your mind-reading thoughts, remind yourself that no one can read minds. Approach people with openness, curiosity, and an external focus so that you can observe their non-verbal as well as verbal behaviors.

Accept that these observations are the best you can do, even though reasonable uncertainty is still a part of the equation.

Fortune Telling
When you catch yourself believing these future-predicting thoughts, remind yourself that the future is uncertain—no one can predict it for sure. It is okay to put your best foot forward and then embrace the uncertainty that is inherent in life.

Catastrophizing
People with phobic social anxiety live in fear of rejection because they worry that rejection will be devastating. This apocalyptic consequence

rarely if ever happens in real life. I often ask my clients who are so fearful of rejection to recall the last time they were catastrophically rejected—certainly everyone is rejected at times. They typically rack their brain, certain that they will come up with something, only to realize that nothing comes to mind. Yet, they often avoid pursuing major social goals because they believe that rejection is catastrophic.

Many of my clients, for example, have never dated out of fear of catastrophic rejection. They imagine that if they were to muster up the courage to finally ask their coworker to lunch, they would be met with a shocked and disgusted expression followed by a dramatically abusive response:

> *"What?! Me go out with you?! Are you kidding me? You are a pathetic little worm who is so completely beneath me that I would not even use you to wipe dog poop from my shoe. Oh my God—what a joke you are! I'm going to tell everyone what you just did. You can never show yourself around here anymore, you loser. I mean, what a friggin' joke!"*

How likely is such a scenario? What would you think about a person who responds like this just for you paying them the compliment of wanting to spend some time with them?

What is the reality of dating rejection?

If someone does not wish to go on a date with you, the "rejection" typically consists of face-saving responses such as:

- "Oh, thank you, but I have plans."
- "That sounds like fun, but I'm currently dating someone."
- "I hope you can find someone to go; I'm just too busy these days."
- "No, thanks."

The bottom line is that life will dish out intermittent portions of rejection to us that can sting and feel disappointing, but it's certainly not unbearable—and the sting does, in fact, ease.

Labeling

We humans are way too complex to be lumped under a single label. For example, in order to be a "failure," we cannot succeed at anything or that label is incorrect. No one fails at everything—in fact, being alive is in itself a success.

Logically speaking, if you spill your drink, you are not a "klutz"— you're just someone who spilled their drink. Similarly, if you give a well-regarded speech, you are not a "success"—you're just someone who gave a well-regarded speech. I know that this is a novel idea, but what if you live life without getting attached to labels?

We all have a little devil on our shoulder whispering the occasional negative label in our ear. You can recognize this as normal and meaningless and avoid getting hooked by that label. You can learn to recognize these thoughts as illogical noise rather than facts.

Negative Filter and Discounting the Positives

What these two categories of thoughts have in common is that they represent biased attention. Perhaps you believe that you are somehow undeserving of positive social interactions. If that is the case, then you may be in the habit of minimizing, discounting, or neglecting to notice when positive exchanges with other people occur.

It is not that I am recommending that you walk around telling yourself how great you are and that everyone admires you. Rather, for logic's sake, I am suggesting that you take in a full range of information. If things are going well socially, then you get to see that your social courage is paying off. If things are not going well, then that is information you need so that you can modify your current strategy, acquire new skills, and/or modify your goals.

Overgeneralizing

If you believe overgeneralizing thoughts such as you always spill your drink or you always put your foot in your mouth at church picnics, then ask yourself—"Really … always?" Most of the time, you will realize after very little consideration that these things happen to you sometimes, and then you can remind yourself that these things, at times, happen to all of us. It is human to be imperfect.

If there are things that happen every single time, however, then new skills or modified goals may be called for.

All-or-Nothing Thinking

If you believe that you must either be a paragon of social sophistication like James Bond or alternatively your social skills are so poor that they would frighten small puppies, then you may be getting hooked by all-or-nothing thoughts. The reality is, however, that life is not black or white, but countless shades of gray in between. While you may never achieve the level of charm of James Bond (it's hard to compete with fictional social perfection), you certainly can interact reasonably effectively most of the time with those nonfictional characters in your life.

You can learn to live with social "gray areas."

Social anxiety may make it difficult to enjoy a social gathering 100 percent. That's okay. If you give it a chance, you probably won't enjoy it zero percent either. The food may taste good (but not gourmet), the music may have a pleasant beat (but be louder than you prefer), and the people may be somewhat friendly (but a few keep their distance). It is okay to allow events in life to be good enough rather than perfect or awful.

Shoulds

Just think for a moment about how much of your life is based on arbitrary "shoulds." As I write this, I am aware of the thought that I "should" finish this book—then I should try to get it published. Logically speaking, however, there really are very few things that SHOULD occur in life. You should take in oxygen, water, and nourishment, and have other basic safety needs met if you want to continue to live. Everything else, however, is a preference, which may be desirable, but does not have to occur. For example, you may prefer that everyone likes you, but you can continue to live and function even if some people do not.

When you get stuck on arbitrary shoulds (for example, "I should be the life of the party!"), you cause yourself additional stress and frustration. Refrain from "shoulding on yourself," as Albert Ellis called it. When you feel stressed in socially anxious situations, ask yourself if you are getting stuck on shoulds. Try taking the pressure off yourself by doing the best you can with things as they are rather than cursing fate that things are not the way they *should* be.

One of the most common "shoulds" I hear from my clients is that they shouldn't be awkward interpersonally. The reality, however, is that humans are an awkward species. The lion on the plains of the Serengeti is not awkward. It lives totally in the moment and is not self-aware the way humans are. Other animals move through life based on instinct and moment-to-moment reactions, rather than dwelling on the past or the future like humans.

Self-awareness means that we are awkward because we think about our life—and not just the present moment either. We live in the past and future in our minds as well. Simply having an awareness of the normal awkwardness in our lives can be quite awkward in itself. This awkwardness begins at birth and is our traveling companion throughout our lives:

- Squeezing through the birth canal—newborn awkward.
- Struggling to take those first steps—stumbling awkward.
- Getting dropped off for your first day of school—new-kid awkward.
- The changes that occur with puberty—squeaky, oily awkward.
- Asking someone on a date—hopeful romantic awkward.
- Your first sexual experience—wow-that-was-over-fast awkward.
- Wearing your graduation gown and silly hat—ceremonially awkward.
- Attending job interviews—power-imbalance awkward.
- Being reprimanded by your boss—have-to-take-it awkward.
- Meeting your romantic partner's parents for the first time—do-they-like-me awkward.
- The tension over dinner after your first fight with your romantic partner—silent awkward.
- Your infant projectile vomits in the produce aisle—hunt-for-paper-towels awkward.

- Your child having a tantrum at a quiet restaurant—frustrated parent awkward.
- Being introduced to your ex's new partner—insecure-hate awkward.
- Undergoing prostate, hernia, or gynecological exams—cold-hands awkward.
- Your first day in your new retirement home—new-kid awkward.
- Purchasing your first box of adult diapers—pharmacy-cashier awkward.

Believing that these experiences should not be awkward or that there is something wrong with you for feeling awkward in these situations runs counter to the reality of the situation. Life is very awkward at times!

You can stay stuck with the "should" belief or simply accept the inherent awkwardness and move forward with life. Since we are all awkward at times, few people are really paying attention to other people's normal life awkwardness. They know that you are awkward at times because they are too.

What is most interesting to me is that when people with high levels of social anxiety hate being awkward and struggle to not be awkward, they actually end up being and feeling even more awkward. In other words, what is most awkward is trying not to be awkward. Embrace your awkwardness and move forward with your social goals.

Personalizing

When you catch yourself believing personalizing thoughts, you are taking the blame for things that may not be your responsibility or are only partially your responsibility. If you are having a conversation with another person, for example, and there is an awkward silence, you are simply responsible for half of that pause. If the conversation is occurring in the context of a work meeting with four people in attendance, then you are only responsible for twenty-five percent of the lull in the conversation. If you are accepting one-hundred percent responsibility ("I'm really blowing it!"), then you are being fooled by a social anxiety thought and can remind yourself of the shared responsibility.

Likewise, if you are giving a talk and someone repeatedly yawns, it might mean many different things other than, "I am boring my audience." Perhaps they slept poorly last night or are depressed or ill. If someone cancels on you an hour before your big date, it could be for any number of reasons other than you did something to offend them.

Unfair Comparisons

Many of my clients with phobic social anxiety attend the local college. When they show up to a large lecture class with a hundred other students, some of them focus their attention on the one person in the room who is unusually attractive, intelligent, popular, and outgoing, and fixate on why they are not just like them. Meanwhile, they fail to notice the rest of the people in the class who are within the average range on these characteristics. If you have been socially avoidant for many years and were born with an introverted nervous system, it is not fair to compare yourself to an extrovert with years of significant social practice. Likewise, it would be unfair to compare yourself to Bruce Lee during your introductory karate class.

If you catch yourself getting hooked by these comparison thoughts, you can remind yourself that you don't have to be anyone but yourself. It is okay to move toward your social goals and to accept being good enough rather than the absolute best.

The Wishing Ritual

Everyone at times wishes that something about themselves were different. The wishing ritual can lead to endless rumination and spinning your wheels rather than moving forward toward your social goals.

If only I were:

- A doctor
- Happier
- Less grumpy
- Less sleepy
- Less dopey
- Less bashful
- And less sneezy …

… then I would ask the princess to the ball!

A more logical approach might be to take steps to change what you can (such as avoidant behaviors or learning and practicing new social skills) and accept those things that can't be changed. Make the best of your current reality and begin taking steps toward your social goals now.

Perfectionism

When you catch yourself striving for perfection, remind yourself that no one and nothing is perfect. Since perfection is a level that humans can never achieve, expecting yourself to be perfect at anything guarantees failure, frustration, and disappointment. Having unrealistic perfectionistic expectations of other people means that they will always let you down and never be good enough. Other people and relationships will continually be frustrating and disappointing.

By embracing the reality of social imperfection, ironically, you may improve your social performance because once the pressure to be perfect is lifted, you'll be less inhibited and more comfortable with yourself. Embracing other people's imperfections with compassion can lead to closer, more intimate relationships as you begin to ease up on unreasonable demands on other people's behaviors.

SUMMARY

Thought Category	Logical Response
Mind Reading	I only know what I can observe. I cannot read minds.
Fortune Telling	No one can predict the future. It's okay to be uncertain.
Catastrophizing	Something may be undesirable, but not unbearable.
Labeling	That's name calling. No one is all good or bad. People are complex and don't have to be globally judged.
Discounting the Positives	I can feel good about the good things I do or that happen.

Negative Filter	Instead of focusing on the one negative thing, I can appreciate the ten positive things.
Overgeneralizing	That's overgeneralizing! There are lots of times that it doesn't happen.
All-or-Nothing Thinking	Life is not black or white, but many shades in between.
Shoulds	I may prefer things to be a certain way, but they don't have to be.
Personalizing	There were other people or events that share responsibility. It's not all my responsibility.
Unfair Comparisons	It's unfair to compare myself to extremes.
Wishing Ritual	It is what it is! I can make the best of it.
Perfectionism	This loses 100 percent of the time because nothing and no one is perfect. It is okay for you and others to be flawed or just good enough socially.

AVOIDING PROBLEMS THAT CAN COME WITH LOGIC

There are a couple of problems that can arise when using logic to cope with social anxiety thoughts. The first is when you don't really believe the thoughts and are using logic in a compulsive way to try to make unpleasant thoughts stay away. We will discuss alternative strategies for coping with brain noise shortly.

The other problem that can arise with the use of logic is that it can come across as cold and judgmental.

- "People at the party don't like me."
  - "I'm mind reading again ... Ugh, why can't I stop this!"
- "I should be as well-spoken as that guy!"
  - "There I go again, shoulding on myself!"

A solution to the use of logic feeling cold and judgmental is to infuse it with compassion.

COMPASSIONATE RESPONSE TO WHAT YOUR BRAIN TELLS YOU

Natalia

Wednesdays were lunch out days with Natalia and her co-workers. Today they had agreed to meet at the food court in the mall. Natalia had loaded up her tray at the salad bar and was casually strolling over to her friends when she suddenly and dramatically tripped over her untied shoelace and tossed her salad across the room. The tray landed with a loud crash, which immediately directed the attention of those in the crowded food court in her direction—just in time to see her awkwardly fall on her face. The room went silent with all eyes upon her. She stood up as quickly as she could, not sure whether to clean up her mess, join her friends, or get back in line for a new lunch. "What a pathetic loser!" she heard her thoughts say. To which she responded, "Wow, that felt uncomfortable, but I'm glad I didn't get hurt. Stuff happens and it's normal to experience embarrassment—it will fade. I certainly don't have to beat myself up."

Here's a novel idea. What if you were unconditionally nice to yourself? Just think for a moment of what this would mean.

If you were to show up late to a meeting, for example, and your automatic thoughts begin scolding you ("You inconsiderate loser!"), why not stick up for yourself like you would if someone was verbally attacking a loved one? As an alternative to your condemning thought, you could tell yourself, "It's okay to make mistakes. No one is perfect.

Maybe if I set my alarm fifteen minutes earlier it would be easier to be on time."

There are emotional consequences to mentally beating yourself up, such as frustration, sadness, or demoralization. By showing yourself compassion instead, you can be bolstered and better prepared to approach the situation differently (if need be) in the moment or in the future.

The relationship that you have with yourself is truly the only constant one in life. You won't always have a parent, friend, or spouse around to pick you up when you are feeling low, but you will always have the person who stares back at you in the mirror. Rather than having an emotionally abusive relationship with that person, wouldn't it be nice to have this relationship be one that is unconditionally accepting?

Practicing compassion includes accepting the fact that life is hard at times and pain will be a regular part of it. Instead of fanning the flames of your pain, you can develop a bias toward seeking to encourage and support yourself, as you would a loved one who is in pain.

If you were brought up by caregivers who lavished you with love and kindness, then self-compassion is easier. If, on the other hand, your caregivers (due to their own problems) showed you little or no compassion or, worse, actively abused you, then learning to be compassionate with yourself will likely feel foreign and perhaps, initially, uncomfortable.

The bottom line is that you were thrown into this life, your family, your environment, and your temperament. None of this was your choice, nor is any of it your fault. Yet, you may be frequently tempted to condemn yourself for the fruit that those seeds bore. While you are reading this book and working on coping and thriving with social anxiety, try to experiment with unconditional positive regard for yourself. Hold onto a bias toward compassion and see what happens. You have little to lose and potentially much to gain by relating to yourself in this way.

Compassion for Your Fellow Humans

Imagine you are rushing home from work to make dinner for your children when you realize that it's Taco Tuesday and you forgot to go to the store to gather the needed taco accessories. You stop by the grocery store and quickly run in and grab what you need and head to the ten-item express aisle. You wait five minutes and then unload your items onto the conveyer. The cashier is a young woman with a scowl on her face. She counts your items and then rudely exiles you from the express line for the grievous error of having eleven items.

Do you automatically (and angrily) label this cashier who has treated you rudely as a "total jerk"?

Perhaps your experience might be more peaceful if you work toward cultivating a sense of compassion toward the cashier rather than condemnation. Here is someone who clearly is in pain and is trying to make the best of it in a flawed way that probably won't win her any friends—which will then increase her pain. Maybe her spouse just served her divorce papers. Perhaps she just received the news that her mother has terminal cancer. Or maybe her boss is sexually harassing her and making her daily life miserable. Regardless, this is a person who has and will experience great pain in life (as we all will). Even if you were on the receiving end of rudeness from her, could you imagine rallying a small amount of compassion for her as a fellow traveler along the rocky path of life?

Ultimately, would you rather be the kind of person who is quick to judge and reject this cashier, or would you prefer to be the kind of person who is quick to move toward compassion, even when someone behaves in a way you dislike? At the end of the day, who would you like to be?

Examples of compassionate responses to social anxiety thoughts:

- Thought: You will embarrass yourself at the party!
  - Self-Compassionate Response: No one's perfect. If I feel embarrassed, I can still pat myself on the back for showing up.
- Thought: Joe is such a jerk for canceling on me last minute!
  - Other-Compassionate Response: I hope everything is all right with Joe.

MERGING LOGIC WITH COMPASSION

Dwayne

Dwayne is up for a promotion at work. He'd like the higher salary and perks, but he's worried about moving into management. At his current job he sits behind his computer all day fixing bad code. The promotion would involve heading up the IT department. That means running meetings and mediating disputes and other social interactions that feel downright uncomfortable. After a sleepless night spent worrying, he concludes, "No one will take me seriously. I'll fail and be utterly humiliated!"

You can combine the logical response with compassion to come up with a Logical and Compassionate Reframe (LCR) to your social anxiety thoughts.

EXERCISE: Logical and Compassionate Reframes

STEP 1: Write down the thoughts that increase your social anxiety.

....

....

No one will take me seriously. I'll fail and be humiliated.

Step 2: Analyze the thoughts. Put them under the microscope, pick them apart, and see where there might be logical errors. What are some more compassionate ways to look at the situation?

You can aid in your analysis by asking yourself questions such as:

- Which categories of anxiety thoughts do my target thoughts fall under?
- What is the evidence that these thoughts are true?
- What is the evidence that these thoughts may be untrue?
- How might an attorney discredit the "true" evidence?
- Would a fair judge find the thoughts true based on the evidence?
- Are you so sure of your thought that you would bet your entire life savings on it? If you would not, why?
- Would those in your life closest to you agree with your thought? If they would not, why?
- What are some other possible ways you could view this situation?
- Do other people share responsibility?
- If these thoughts were true, would it be possible to cope, or even accept the situation and make your life as good as possible anyway? Are there skills you could learn and practice or other changes that you could make, if your thoughts were true, that would improve the situation?

Dwayne's thought analysis

My thoughts seem to fall under the categories of fortune telling and catastrophizing.

Evidence that these thoughts might be true:

- I haven't started and I'm already so worried I'm losing sleep.

- I've never taken a leadership position before.
- Sometimes my coworkers don't seem to take my input seriously.
- I just don't feel like I can do it.

Evidence that these thoughts might NOT be true:

- I have worked for my company for ten years and know the ins and outs of the IT department better than anyone.
- Every year I get glowing reviews of my work.
- They would not have offered me the promotion if they did not think I could handle it.
- People in my department seek out my input on a regular basis already.

Refuting the "true" evidence:

- Just because I am worrying now does not mean that I won't be able to do the job; I can't predict the future.
- Just because I have never managed people before does not mean I won't be able to pick up those skills after the promotion ... I don't have to be perfect.
- A lot of my coworkers do take my input seriously and the others will likely begin to take my input seriously when I am their boss.
- Emotional reasoning is not good evidence that I can't do it.

The evidence itself does not indicate that I'll fail and be humiliated.

I would not bet my life savings on my thoughts being true—there just is not a good reason why I would fail and be humiliated, and there is some evidence that I may do well. People who know me well would say that I am a hard worker and that I have paid my dues and made myself valuable to the company—they would say I can do it.

Other ways I could view this situation:

- If the promotion does not work out, I can always ask to return to my current job.
- I tend to get nervous with big changes, but they tend to work out most of the time.
- I wouldn't be the first person to fail and it does not necessarily mean humiliation.
- Better to try and fail than not try at all.

If I were to fail, other people who would share the responsibility include:

- My bosses who promoted me without proper training and support.
- My employees if they don't listen to me.
- Worst case, if these thoughts turn out to be true, it does not mean it's the end of the world. I could always get a new job, extra training, and take concrete steps to cope with and learn from the experience.

STEP 3: What would someone who is absolutely compassionate say?

Imagine someone who is unconditionally compassionate. Pretend that they know the complexities of your upbringing, struggles, and current life situation. How might they respond to your thoughts in a way that is completely understanding and compassionate?

....

....

....

....

....

....

....

....

....

Change can be tough for anyone. It is normal and okay to feel nervous and have self-doubting thoughts. You have every right to go for what you want, even if you have doubts. If it doesn't work out, it is okay to feel disappointed and awkward around the office for a while. You wouldn't have to beat yourself up and instead you could actively work to cope and move past this.

Step 4: Bringing it together into a Logical and Compassionate Reframe (LCR)

Now take the essence of what you learned in steps 2 and 3 and write a response (your LCR) to your initial anxiety thoughts. Keep it brief and to the point.

....

....

....

....

....

It is normal and okay to feel worried and to have doubts. No one can predict the future and there is no evidence that I'll fail. Even if I do, I can cope and move forward with life—it is highly unlikely to be catastrophic.

PUTTING LCR INTO PRACTICE

It is most helpful to pick apart social anxiety thoughts in times of unhurried reflection. Remember, the goal is to downgrade these thoughts from beliefs to simply brain noise. For example, if you want to date, but believe the thought that no one would want to date you, the goal is to pick apart this belief that is stopping you from moving forward with dating.

This is not an activity to undertake during the fearful social interaction. When you are interacting with others, the focus should be on being in the moment, in the interaction—not sidelined in your head doing logical and compassion analysis.

When you are in the moment and feeling frightened, it can be helpful to be your own cheerleader: "I can do it, way to go, stick with it, remember to focus externally, let go of struggling, it's okay to feel the anxiety and let it run its course … " and so on. Leave the in-depth analysis for another time.

What if, after analysis, the thoughts turn out to be true?

Sometimes your social anxiety belief may be accurate. Maybe you are persistently rejected in a particular situation. In the chapter on obstacles and setbacks, you will learn about what to do when anxiety is right. For example:

1. Engage in active problem solving.
2. Modify your goal. (Lower your objective to Duke or
    Earl rather than King of England, perhaps.)
3. Learn and practice skills intended to increase your likelihood
    of success. (Read a book on management strategies,
    attend a public speaking group like Toastmasters, or watch
    some videos on contemporary dating etiquette.)
4. Always return to basic compassion for your struggles and
    seek to "de-catastrophize" the situation. (It is okay to fail at
    things and feel disappointed. I am still a worthwhile person.
    It's not the end of the world, I can learn from my mistakes.)

I've done the LCR and I really don't believe the thoughts completely, but the thoughts don't stop!

> They haunt me when I go to a party. They are the watchful chaperone when I am on a date. They try to talk over me

during presentations ... my social anxiety thoughts follow me wherever I go!

So far you have learned to become aware of your social anxiety thoughts and when these thoughts rise to the level of beliefs that hold you back. Then you can use logical and compassionate reframes as a kind of mental yoga to stretch your thinking to begin to see things from a new perspective. However, the thoughts don't stop—they never stop completely. The human brain is a noisy place. Your better-safe-than-sorry brain will continue to produce anxiety thoughts whether you believe them or not.

The Buddhists call the ever-present stormy swirl of thoughts in the background of our consciousness the "Monkey Mind."

Exercise: Peeking at your Monkey Mind

Set a timer for two minutes. Now close your eyes and notice the commotion taking place in your consciousness. Are you seeing one reasonable thought after another, slowly moving single-file across your mind in a neat and orderly line?

If you are like most people, you probably did not see a mere trickle of orderly thoughts. You likely experienced a torrential flood of thoughts of near-biblical proportions. Welcome to the Monkey Mind. At times it probably feels more like a wild gang of over-caffeinated monkeys with ADHD, rather than just a single monkey!

The day our mind gets purged from the onslaught of thoughts is the day we die. No sooner. No amount of LCR will rid you of this marauding monkey army, but you can learn to coexist and even thrive despite the mayhem.

COPING AND THRIVING WITH SOCIAL ANXIETY "BRAIN NOISE"

The Thought Vendors

You are a tourist in the frenzied marketplace of thoughts. The "thought vendors" take a look at you and swarm—eager to make a quick sale.

Thoughts for sale! Get them while they're hot! Ah, you— Sir/Madam, may I interest you in a thought today? Come on, this is a very important thought. Take a listen ...

PEOPLE THINK I AM A FOOL
You really must buy this thought. Come on, it really is a very compelling thought! On sale today—a special price just for you! It will only cost you ...

FRIENDSHIP, LOVE, AND JOYFUL MOMENTS
What a super-fantastic deal this is—just for you! Come on, it's such a fascinating thought at such a small price.

You've stumbled upon this lively bazaar and the vendors are excitedly trying to make a sale. You are surrounded and feeling overwhelmed. You quickly assess your options.

- You could buy the thought at the asking price—though you're not sure there is space for that item in your life and the cost seems quite steep. If you buy the thought, you believe it and live your life according to it.
- Alternatively, you could look for a gap in the crowd and try to run away from the vendors. If you do, however, they will chase you and block you from your social destination.
- You wonder about trying to push the vendors away or even attempting to fight them off. The commotion,

however, will just attract the attention of more vendors who will join the crowd and block you from your social destination.

- Perhaps you could appeal to reason and explain to them that you just don't believe in their product and therefore don't want it. Engaging them in discussion, however, will just further encourage their aggressive sales tactics. They may never tire of trying to sell you the thought if you keep engaging with them.
- You could get sneaky and try to hide from the vendors behind alcohol, food, and other distractions. This may even work for a while, but the vendors will keep looking for you and eventually will find you and pick up where they left off. And, while you are hiding, you are not moving toward your social destination.

It begins to feel hopeless. You are trapped.

Suddenly you have a flash of insight. You realize that thought vendors are part of life. In order to continue your journey toward your social destination, you decide to try a radically different approach.

You greet the vendors with a smile and allow them to walk with you toward your social destination. You let them talk, but you don't take part, other than calmly acknowledging that they are talking. You put one foot in front of the other and keep moving forward. The vendors are just doing their job; you can understand that, so you accept that they will always be there, but you can be street smart and not buy thoughts that you don't really want and certainly don't need.

You can learn to peacefully coexist with the thought vendors.

Accepting the presence of the anxiety thoughts rather than fighting a losing battle

Instead of focusing on the hopeless task of getting rid of social anxiety thoughts, what if you could learn to treat them as background noise, rather than as a signal to take action (or avoid action)? What if you could accept the presence of social anxiety thoughts and coexist in relative peace, rather than spending your time and mental resources in the futile struggle to get rid of these thoughts, which paradoxically only serves to make them louder?

In recent years, therapists and researchers have looked to the Far East at ancient mental health strategies to help with modern human suffering. Today, the application of mindfulness and acceptance-based coping strategies play a significant role in mainstream mental health practices.

What these strategies assert is that accepting without judgment the presence of thoughts and feelings as temporary human experiences leads to a reduction in suffering. Alternatively, struggling to get rid of these experiences tends to increase suffering (and often intensifies the experiences themselves).

Utilizing principles of Eastern traditions merged with more contemporary behavioral therapy, Dr. Steven C. Hayes developed Acceptance and Commitment Therapy (ACT) as a psychological system designed to reduce suffering while taking concrete steps toward one's valued activities. Instead of wasting precious moments of your life in a never-ending struggle against discomfort, he recommends that you accept without judgment some inevitable unpleasantness in life. The goal is to "defuse" or detach from the discomfort, and instead, refocus on behaving in ways that are consistent with what you really value in life. So, instead of staying home to avoid social anxiety, you let go of battling or running from the anxiety and move ever forward, keeping your eye on the social prize you are seeking.

The goal of defusion is to learn to become the observer of the unpleasantness, not the unpleasantness itself. For example:

Fighting the Discomfort
"I am miserable at this party! I just hate being so awkward. Trying to make small talk is unbearable. I'm going to screw this up any minute. People think I am pathetic. I'm starting to sweat and my heart is racing ... I have to get out of here!"

Acceptance and Defusion

"I am aware that I feel uncomfortable. I am aware of thoughts that I am awkward and will be rejected. I am noticing my heart rate increasing and my palms are moistening. I am aware of an urge to leave ... AND I will choose to stay here and start conversations with three people."

Notice that defusion is not about getting rid of your experiences. Rather it involves mindfully acknowledging your experiences as experiences without fusing with them. (For example, "I am such a loser" versus "I am aware of the thought that I am a loser.")

DEFUSION STRATEGIES

There are a number of strategies and techniques that ACT and other approaches utilize to assist in defusion. The ultimate goal is to take the power away from these thoughts so that they no longer torture you or influence your social choices. Here are some of my favorites.

Describe, don't judge

You are not your thoughts; you are the observer of your thoughts. So, observe them. When you feel the pull to fuse with social anxiety thoughts, describe your experience:

- I am aware of the thought, "I am a loser."
- I am aware of the urge to tighten up and fight the anxiety.
- I am aware of the urge to flee.

By doing this, you are taking a step back and observing your experience with some distance and perspective. Then you will be better able to choose your response rather than fusing with the social anxiety thought ("Nobody wants me here!") and avoiding a situation that may have furthered your social goals.

Chessboard

This metaphor involves imagining a chessboard that stretches out in infinite directions. On one side of the chessboard are the social anxiety thoughts:

- "No one here likes you."
- "You are boring them."
- "Blushing would be catastrophic."
- "You shouldn't be here."

On the other side are your chess pieces:

- "I *am* a likable person."
- "I am *not* boring them."
- "No one can see me blush."
- "I *should* be here."

You can imagine being locked into a never-ending game of chess with anxiety. Anxiety makes a move, then you counter. Sometimes anxiety gains the advantage, sometimes you hold anxiety off, and sometimes you gain a temporary advantage. The game, however, plays on … and on … and on!

What if, instead of a constant battle of wills against anxiety, you realize that you can be the chessboard itself? The noise of the game continues, but it is happening above you and you don't have to participate anymore. In fact, you don't even have to feed it by being an engaged spectator. The noise can be present, *and* you can choose to refocus on the social goal at hand while letting the game go on in the background without your participation.

Broken Radio Station

This analogy has you imagine a very unpleasant radio station, "Social Rejection Forecast Radio," which has only one focus: predicting catastrophic social rejection. It might play something like this:

"I'm Doom Gloom and thank you for tuning into SRFR where you get your social rejection news 24/7. Today in the news, you really looked awkward during the meeting at work and no one liked you. Later in the morning you stumbled over your words and everyone now thinks you are weird. In sports today, you looked like a total buffoon at the gym. Now for weather, you have a 100 percent chance of falling dramatically on the ice later today and no one will help you up … Breaking news! We need to interrupt this broadcast and take you live to the middle of your work presentation. You look stupid and will probably get fired! Next up, which new cellphone games are best to play while you hide from the world?"

As silly as this may seem, it represents the frequent internal experience of many people with high levels of social anxiety and, at times, all of us. You could spend the rest of your life fighting your brain to try to get this station taken off the air, but think about how much time and energy goes into this futile fight. Think of all the better ways you could direct your resources. Imagine that your radio is broken and the station can't be changed or turned off no matter how hard you try. In fact, when you try to turn off the radio or at least turn the volume down, it inadvertently cranks up the volume instead!

Instead of focusing on turning off the radio, what if you just let it be? What if you learned to live with the station droning on in the background, letting it be background noise and refocus on moving toward your social goals instead? Think about how often you do this with other "noises" such as your air conditioning, refrigerator, or the crickets chirping outside your home. Think about how many noises you already coexist with and the amazing fact that, at times, even though the noises are still present, you no longer hear them!

Computer Pop-up Scam

Who hasn't had the experience of being online when an urgent-looking pop-up "notification" flashes onto their computer screen? Maybe it says that you have just been infected by a computer virus and to "click here" to have it removed. Perhaps the pop-up announces that you have just won something valuable. If you click on these notifications, however, odds are you have just graciously held the door open for a malevolent virus to infest your computer.

Imagine you are making a presentation at school or work. In the middle of the presentation you become aware of pop-up alerts flashing across your mind.

This isn't going well!	They don't like you!	*What a loser!*
Click here for "help"	Click here for "help"	Click here for "help"

"Clicking" on these notifications means that you shift some of your mental focus onto the content of these thoughts, perhaps behaving as if they are true. Maybe you stop making eye contact and rush through the rest of your presentation.

If you click on these types of notifications, you are likely to get sucked up into your head. Rather than focusing on communicating your intended information to your classmates or colleagues, your focus becomes internal, nitpicking what you just said, how you look, and rehearsing the perfect thing to say next. Your inner world becomes an imaginary, skewed, nightmarish version of what is actually happening externally—right in front of you.

Rather than clicking on these pop-ups, acknowledge your awareness of these notifications without getting sucked into the content—refocus externally. We all have to live with pop-ups in our brains, but we have some control over how often we click on them. Sometimes these notifications will be clever and persuasive and you will be tempted to click on them. Reducing the number of times you click on pop-ups can be a significant improvement.

Let go, let God

For the spiritually inclined, turning control and responsibility over the social anxiety thoughts to their higher power can be a helpful strategy for defusing from these thoughts. If it falls within your belief system, feel free to use it. Some people will simply visualize the anxious thoughts floating upward as they acknowledge that their higher power is looking out for their best interest and they don't need to concern themselves with the noise of these thoughts.

Anxiety as a Person

One of my go-to strategies for defusion from anxious thoughts is to personify them—that is, to talk about anxiety as if it were an actual person (you probably have seen this throughout the book so far). This facilitates defusion by allowing you to say, "Oh, that's just anxiety talking," rather than immediately latching onto the thoughts that arise automatically. Here are some ways to personify anxiety.

Imagine anxiety as the …

Competitor:

Anxiety is the eager competitor—sports, poker, board games, you name it! Anxiety wants to win at all costs and is willing to stoop to sneaky tricks in order to win. Anxiety has bet that it can make you back down from talking to the attractive person at the party. Are you going to let anxiety win?

Bad Coach:

The bad coach attempts to "improve" your performance through bullying and intimidation ("Move, you stupid piece of *&%#!"). We all have the bad coach in our head sometimes. The good news is that you no longer need to dignify him with a response. Let the bad coach yell in the background, but refuse to play on this coach's team.

Humorous Character:

Do you know what really helps some people to defuse from anxiety thoughts? Find them hilarious! Who is the goofball character from TV or movies who makes you laugh? Imagine anxiety speaking in that voice. Pick the character of your choice. For example, the Dr. Evil in your head says, *"Leave this party now or pay the price … one million dollars!"* Other favorites, Homer Simpson (Okay, any Simpson character will do!), Stewie Griffin (again, pick your favorite Griffin!), the Count from *Sesame Street,*

Eric Cartman from *South Park*, George Costanza from *Seinfeld* (or Larry David, if you are so inclined), Michael Scott from *The Office*, Bugs Bunny … take your pick! Put their voice onto your automatic thoughts using that wonderful imagination of yours. Then, instead of those thoughts hooking you and controlling you, you can simply acknowledge them with, "Oh Homer, there you go again!"

Obnoxious Debate Partner:

While logic and reason can at times be helpful to modify a faulty belief, they can be pointless if you are trying to change the mind of someone who is not open to other points of view. The more you press this person to believe what you believe, the more persistently they resist. Ever try convincing someone to support the presidential candidate that they are currently passionately opposed to? How well does that work out for you? Likewise, trying to convince social anxiety of the "safety" of a particular social encounter can be frustrating and fruitless.

> Anxiety: "No one here likes you!"
> You: "That is not true."
> Anxiety: "It is true!"
> You: "People are talking to me and they seem friendly."
> Anxiety: "They just feel sorry for you."
> You: "But they invited me, even when they did not have to."
> Anxiety: "They just did that because they feel sorry for you. They did not want you to actually show up."
> You: "That's not true!"
> Anxiety: "How do you know for sure?"
> You: "Because they seem friendly."
> Anxiety: "How do you know for sure, 100 percent, that they want you here?"
> You: " … "
> Anxiety: "Check and mate!"

The LCR that you learned about in the previous section of the book is designed to raise reasonable doubt for you, not to strive for the hundred-percent certainty that anxiety demands. Ultimately, there is no effective logical comeback to a debate partner who insists on you proving something 100 percent.

So, instead of engaging in a debate that you can never win, notice that anxiety is trying to suck you into a no-win argument. Don't take the bait. Simply acknowledge that anxiety is trying to pull you in and refocus on the social task at hand.

The Seducer:

You probably recognize anxiety when it is screaming danger messages at you. ("Get the heck out of this party! You are making a fool of yourself!") It may be much easier to defuse from anxiety when it is so noisy that its game is unmistakable. There is another side to anxiety, however, that the analogy of the Seducer represents.

The Seducer won't yell and raise alarm bells. Instead, the Seducer gently sidles up to you, puts its arm around you and pretends to be your friend. The Seducer may even speak to you with great compassion. It might sound something like this:

The Seducer: "Tough day at work, huh?"
You: "Yeah, I am a little tired."
The Seducer: "You know what sounds nice? How about staying in and relaxing tonight? We can zap some microwave popcorn and watch a movie. Doesn't that sound pleasant?"
You: "It sounds great, but I have that party to go to. I really want to challenge myself socially."
The Seducer: "You could go to the party, but think about how unpleasant it will be. You've had such a hard day and there will always be other parties. Why don't you treat yourself to some quality you-time tonight? You can make up for it another time."
You: "But I really want to work on my social goals."
The Seducer: "I get that ... and good for you, by the way. But how about staying in tonight and resting up and going after those social goals when you are more refreshed? You deserve some downtime."

> You: "You know, you are right. Me-time sounds great! I'll catch the next party."
>
> The Seducer: "Good for you! Oh and sorry for the social isolation and loneliness ... oops!"

Here's the problem—the seduction dance will continue and continue and continue. You will be fooled into going for short-term comfort at the expense of long-term neglect of important social goals. By recognizing the Seducer's tactics, you can defuse from the noise and move forward with your social goals.

You might respond like this: "I am aware of anxiety trying to seduce me into avoiding my social goals and I am aware of the urge to give in—AND I choose to go to the party anyway." Having the psychological flexibility to feel like giving in to avoidance while choosing to push forward anyway is key to social courage.

Frightened Child:

Some people prefer a different type of personification. Instead of seeing anxiety as working against them, they prefer to think of anxiety in a less malevolent analogy for their preferred defusion strategy. As with everything in this book, do what works best for you.

You can think of anxiety as a frightened two-year-old child. The child does not want to feel scared, but does anyway. It is natural for small children, when frightened, to fuss and try to convince caretakers to remove them from the situation they find so scary. You can logically explain to a two-year-old that the lion roaring behind the steel bars at the zoo cannot get to them, but the logic is irrelevant—the child feels in danger and wants to leave no matter what you say. They may be just too young to understand logic. If you flee the zoo, the child does not get to learn that the situation was safe and will continue to be frightened.

The Frightened Child at the Party

Frightened Child: I wanna go home. No one here likes me.

You:	It is important to be here for your social development.
Frightened Child:	Time to go. Let's go now!
You:	What is the evidence that no one here likes you?
Frightened Child:	I WANNA GO NOW!

Your defusion strategy may be to mentally acknowledge that the Frightened Child is getting feisty. You can let the child cry, whine, or even throw a tantrum. You don't need to engage or obey the commands of this child or get into a logical discussion. You can mentally acknowledge the child's fear and then model bravery in the face of fear—you certainly wouldn't want to teach your children to avoid social challenges.

Driving the Bus

This is one of my favorite ACT metaphors. Sometimes social anxiety thoughts seem less like a one-on-one conversation and more like you versus a busload of noisy and pushy passengers. Imagine that you are the driver of that bus. Your job is to drive the bus to your destination.

Here is the big question—Do YOU choose your destination (more friends, romantic life, fun social activities, career advancement, and so forth) or do you want your passengers to bully you into changing directions by shouting at you? If you change your direction based on the noise your passengers make, then you are no closer to your social goal. The passengers' only power is to make noise. If you are willing to continue the drive toward your goals *with* those rowdy passengers still on board, then you are free to move toward those goals.

The aspiring author was driving the bus toward his destination of writing a book. One of the passengers in the back began yelling, "No one will want to read this!" Another passenger then chimed in with, "You know you'll never finish it. Why bother?" The aspiring author became aware of a third passenger yelling to him, "You are a terrible writer!" He knew that if he just stopped trying to write his book, the annoying passengers would quiet down—simple as that.

> However, it had been his goal for many years to write a book and he did not want to let the passengers on the bus make him change his direction. "Okay, I want to write this book," he said to himself. "Therefore, the noisy passengers are welcome to come along as I drive toward my destination."

EXERCISE: What is one of your social goals that you would really like to drive your bus toward?

....

....

What are your passengers saying?

Passenger 1: ....

Passenger 2: ....

Passenger 3: ....

....

You now have a choice. You can quiet your passengers by stopping the bus or you can continue to drive toward your destination *with* your passengers on board while they speak their minds.

Check which choice you will make:

- ☐ I will stop my bus so the passengers quiet down.
- ☐ I will continue driving toward my destination with noisy passengers on board.

The Power of Paradox: Give me more thoughts!

Social anxiety thoughts can certainly feel unwanted. However, the paradox is that the more you don't want the thoughts, the more you have them. Hate them and you have them more. Fight with them and the volume turns way up. If you've ever had an annoying song stuck in your head, it works the same way. If a social anxiety thought is not allowed, then you are fused with it—locked in a struggle you are destined to lose.

Psychologist Dr. Reid Wilson has written about how to break this unfortunate fusion pattern. We have discussed accepting social anxiety thoughts as a normal part of life. You aren't getting rid of them. However, you can move toward greater defusion from these thoughts if you not only accept the presence of social anxiety thoughts, but actually demand that they be there.

It may seem at times that anxiety is trying to control you.

> Anxiety: "If you don't leave that party, I am going to tell you scary things and then I will give you uncomfortable feelings."
> It wants you to say, "Oh no, not scary thoughts and feelings—I'll leave!"
> What if, instead, you stood up to anxiety?
> Anxiety: "If you don't leave that party, I am going to tell you scary things and then I will give you uncomfortable feelings."
> You: "Okay, bring on the thoughts. I'm ready to coexist with them."
> Anxiety: "You are foolish. Everyone is sickened by you, and you will be humiliated."
> You: "Is that it? Is that the best you've got? Come on, dude, after all I've avoided for you, *that* is the best you can come up with? You can do better than that—I demand that you think me some scarier thoughts. Come on, bring them on!"

Try it. You just might find that this defusion strategy takes the wind out of social anxiety's sails.

Thought Exposure

Repeating any thought over and over again for a prolonged period of time can be a useful defusion strategy. Test it out and see for yourself.

EXERCISE: Take an everyday, non-threatening word such as "paper," "car," or "brunch"—you pick. Now, find some time when you are alone and begin repeating your word, out loud, repeatedly for three minutes. Notice what happens to the word over that time. It starts to sound like meaningless noise.

Next, you could try a word that you find uncomfortable to say out loud (four-letter words are frequently selected, but you could also use the name of your least favorite politician). Repeat the word out loud for five to ten minutes. Allow yourself no distractions (music, TV, smart phone)—just monotonous repetition. What happens? You likely had some experience of defusion with the word.

Finally, take one of social anxiety's thoughts that tend to tweak your emotions and lead you to fuse with it. Try repeating that thought for up to thirty minutes (or until bored silly). Did it lose some of its kick?

Optionally, you can combine this with changing how you verbalize the thought. For example:

• Singing the thought to the tune of a song. ("Row, Row, Row Your Boat" becomes "I, I, suck so much, I really, really do. I suck so very much, I'll never be liked by you.")
• You can repeat the thought really quickly or reaaaally slowly.
• You could hum the thought.
• You could use a different voice inflection (much older or much younger, monotone, foreign accent, and so forth).

Experiment with various defusion strategies to see which works best for you.

Radical Acceptance: Welcoming the thought

Instead of struggle, simply welcome the thought and invite it to freely run its course. When it pops up, instead of starting a power struggle or quest for certainty, just simply say, "Hello," and leave it at that.

If you want to try something a bit more advanced, take a deep breath and breathe in the thought (and subsequent emotions) and breathe out any resistance to the thought—repeatedly.

Normalizing the Thought

When you become aware of social anxiety thoughts, remind yourself that these are the normal (albeit unpleasant) types of thoughts that we humans with better-safe-than-sorry brains have. Remind yourself that the problem is never the social anxiety thought itself, but your reaction to the thoughts.

Tug-of-War

Imagine anxiety has tricked you into playing an endless game of tug-of-war. When anxiety tosses you a thought of potential social rejection, it is offering you one end of a rope to hold onto as the tug-of-war commences.

Anxiety demands, "Play with me!" You are ready and willing to play. You pick up the rope and begin the game. Anxiety pulls hard and warns you, "Don't let go … all is lost if you let go. If you let go, you will be rejected and humiliated. Whatever you do, don't let go; don't ever let go. PLAY WITH ME!"

Anxiety tugs: "You are not good enough. People don't like you. You are going to embarrass yourself."

You tug back, either struggling to get rid of the thoughts or to get certainty that they are not true. Tugging back leads you to fuse with the thought. Anxiety continues to yank on the rope.

After a while, you get tired; it is a very strenuous endeavor. While you are vigorously playing this epic game of tug-of-war with social anxiety, you are laser-focused on not losing the game—not dropping the rope. Here's the problem: you can't focus on playing this game with social anxiety and at the same time focus on moving toward friendships, romantic relationships, or even focusing on the person you are talking to at the party or the people attending your meeting. You can only focus on the game.

What do you think would happen if you dropped the rope? Anxiety would most likely demand that you pick it back up—"Play with me!" You might even be tempted to pick it back up. What if you crossed your arms and refused to play further. Eventually, social anxiety's urging will weaken. You can reject the call to fuse with the thoughts by picking the rope back up.

The next time you are in an uncomfortable social situation, try imagining that social anxiety is there, trying to get you to pick up the rope and play. What will you choose to do?

Naming the Thinking Trap

In an earlier section, we discussed the categories of social anxiety thoughts people have. Rather than challenging the logic behind these thoughts when you notice one pop up, you could just identify the category and leave it at that—letting the thought be.

* "He does not like you" becomes … *There is a Mind Reading thought.*
* "You'll mess up" becomes … *There is a Fortune Telling thought.*
* "This silence means you're blowing it" becomes … *There is a Personalization thought.*
* "If you mess up, you'll never live it down" becomes … *There is a Catastrophizing thought.*

You would not analyze the thought to see the evidence for and against its veracity. Instead, you passively notice and label the thought, then return to the social task at hand—keeping your eye on the prize.

Make Your Own Defusion Strategy

You've now learned a number of defusion strategies. You can also feel free to make your own based on your own life and interests.

* If you are a Star Wars fan, you can think about the anxious thoughts as being from the dark side and you can respond in the way of your favorite Jedi knight.
* If you are a plumber, perhaps the thoughts can be like the leaky faucet you might hear day after day.
* If you are a martial artist, how could you deftly evade getting punched by the thoughts?
* If you are an athlete, how could you respond to the "other team's trash talk"?

What is important is that your strategy allows you to coexist with social anxiety thoughts without judgment or struggle.

MINDFULNESS TRAINING: TURBOCHARGING DEFUSION

Over the past decade or two, the amount of research demonstrating the benefits of mindfulness training has exploded worldwide. The ancient practice of mindfulness, which was somewhat of a fringe new age tradition in the west in the 1960s, is now considered state-of-the-art mainstream psychological (and medical) treatment.

Mindfulness practice is not about achieving enlightenment or joining a new religion. You don't need to shave your head and put on a robe. Rather, it is a mental attention and defusion exercise that involves directing your focus at something (dishes, hiking, eating, breathing, stream of thoughts—anything) and when your mind inevitably wanders, you passively acknowledge this without judgment. You practice defusing from the content of the distraction. At the same time, you practice living in the present moment with your experience.

One used to have to train with a mindfulness teacher to learn this practice. Now, however, there are an abundance of apps on your phone or videos on the internet that can train you in this type of exercise. If you could take a pill that improved your attention and ability to cope with stress and anxiety, as well as potentially increased your lifespan … if it did not cost anything and had zero side effects, would you take this pill?

The basic exercise is to focus on something, acknowledge without judgment when your mind wanders, and gently redirect your attention back to your focal point. If you choose your breath to focus on, it might look something like:

> Breath … breath … breath … my boss hates me … there is thought … back to breath … breath … breath … breath … the party is going to be too uncomfortable … there is thought … back to breath … breath … breath …

Common Mistake: Using defusion strategies as a "sneaky trick" to make social anxiety thoughts go away

One of the most common mistakes people make with defusion strategies is to conclude that they've failed if the social anxiety thoughts don't go away after practicing acceptance of and defusion from them. But if your goal is to get rid of these thoughts, you've just ensured them a place of prominence in your mind.

Remember, the goal is to peacefully coexist with the social anxiety thoughts, rather than abolish them. They're just brain noise ... and it's normal and okay for them to be there. Just keep putting one foot in front of the other and move ever closer toward your social goals.

Overview of Coping and Thriving with Social Anxiety Thoughts

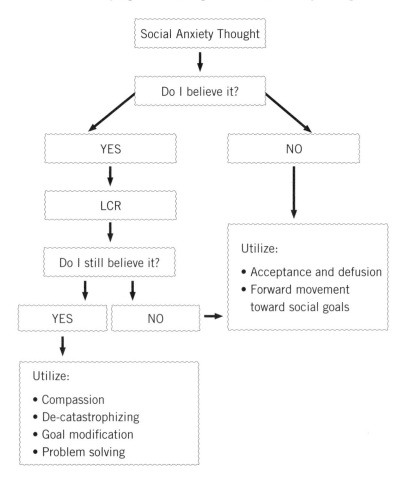

Clean vs. Dirty Social Discomfort

How to stop fighting your feelings and move forward with your life

Susan

Susan had always depended on her older sister for a social life. As a child, she would tag along with her sister and her sister's friends, but would never seek out friendships of her own. Though at times she felt almost like part of this group, she was painfully aware that she was missing out on having friends of her own.

Eventually her sister and her sister's friends graduated from high school and moved away for college, leaving Susan friendless and alone. Her parents encouraged her to get involved in school activities to meet other people, but Susan always declined, giving the excuse that in a year she'd be going off to college—so what was the point of making friends now? In reality, though, she was very nervous to meet new people on her own. She tried in vain to get her social needs met by keeping up with her sister and her sister's friends' social media updates. Her senior year in high school turned into an unbearably lonely time.

> When it was her turn to go off to college, she held high hopes of having a fresh start. She was determined to have that social life she always wanted. She even dared to hope she would meet the love of her life.
>
> Now here Susan was, a nineteen-year-old freshman sitting alone in her dorm room on yet another Saturday night, listening to the sounds of merriment of her fellow dormmates in the common area just outside of her room. She longed to join the fun, but felt way too nervous to do so, so resigned herself instead to another date with Netflix.

Whereas anxiety thoughts are noise of the mind, anxiety feelings are noise of the body. Along with social anxiety feelings, people often experience an increased heart rate and respiration, sweating, blushing, numbness or tingling in the hands or feet, tight muscles, feeling hot or cold, having the sense of being in a dream or detached from present experience, and so forth. Such feelings can definitely grab your attention!

THE UNCOMFORTABLE REALITY OF HUMAN EMOTIONS: THERE IS NO "CURE"!

We humans experience a range of emotions day to day. Some of them can feel downright unpleasant. Take a moment and think of the things that you have tried to do to forever rid yourself of experiencing socially anxious feelings. Maybe you have tried breathing exercises or perhaps you are adept at looking at the brighter side of life. Some people have even tried to yoga their way out of experiencing social anxiety.

EXERCISE: What types of things have you attempted in order to make social anxiety go away for good?

1. ....
2. ....
3. ....
4. ....
5. ....

Yet, here you are—still human and still experiencing socially anxious feelings. The irony is that now you are likely having thoughts such as, "*I am a failure when it comes to getting rid of social anxiety!*" You may even have anxiety about not being able to get rid of anxiety.

No doubt there are some things that have probably worked quite well for you in the short term such as avoiding social situations or using substances to numb out the feelings—yet, here you are.

That's not to say that you cannot take steps to reduce the actual intensity of socially anxious feelings. You likely can—to some degree. You are just fighting a losing battle if your goal is the complete annihilation of a normal human emotion.

But other people don't look anxious in social situations

Just because you don't see the social anxiety in others does not mean they aren't experiencing it. Anxiety most often occurs beneath the skin (inside your mind and body) and may not be reflected in external signs or behaviors, or as what poker players might call a "tell." The most socially uncomfortable people I work with also tend to be the ones who appear the most socially bored and aloof. They go to great lengths to hide any sign of their anxiety and have often gotten very good at it, typically much better than they think. So, remember the old adage, don't judge a book by its cover, because even though the cover may say "Dictionary," the inside might hold a heart-pounding thriller!

Try not to compare what's happening inside of you to what you see on the outside of other people.

CLEAN DISCOMFORT VS. DIRTY DISCOMFORT

Buddhists talk a lot about pain and suffering in life. They speak of the pain you would experience after being struck by an arrow that has been fired into you from afar. The discomfort that this causes you is outside of your control. It hurts. Anyone who gets struck by that arrow in such a way will feel the pain that it brings. The Buddha spoke of a second arrow, however, which is a reaction to the first arrow. When you judge and condemn the pain you feel from the first arrow ("Bad me; I am such a loser for feeling this pain"), you are now experiencing pain from a second arrow. This wound, though, is self-inflicted.

Clean Discomfort

Another way to look at the first arrow is to consider it "clean discomfort"—discomfort that is normal and appropriate for the context. This might be due to discomfort after a poor night's sleep, loss of a loved one, stress at work, death of a friend, or giving a sales pitch to an important prospective new client. In these situations (and countless others), at least some discomfort is universally experienced.

As I am writing this today, I am experiencing a common cold. I am aware of:

- Sinus pressure and headache
- Itchy watery eyes
- Sore throat
- Fatigue
- A preference to feel differently
- The urge to go back to bed rather than complete a bit of writing before going to work

This is clean discomfort. If you were infected by the same cold virus, you would feel similarly. Notice that my description of the clean discomfort is not a judgment. I just feel uncomfortable.

Dirty Discomfort

The second arrow is the judgmental condemnation and resistance to the first arrow.

Instead of allowing the experience of my cold to be present and run its course, I could shoot myself with a second arrow:

> I can't stand being sick! Why me? I've got to get over this. When is this going to be gone? I hate this so much! Oh, cruel fate cast down upon me by the gods of bacteria, why hast thou cursed me so?

Another way to conceptualize this second arrow is as "dirty discomfort" that gets poured on top of a "clean discomfort." The dirty discomfort involves a struggle against the clean discomfort and leads to a significantly higher level of total discomfort.

Let's say that your beloved dog dies. Like most people, you likely will feel intense and unpleasant feelings of grief. That is the clean discomfort. The dirty discomfort is your attempt at emotional avoidance. It is how you reject and try to fight off the feelings. The dirty discomfort is the bucket of gasoline you poor onto your emotional fire to try to put it out. It garners the opposite result—you feel much worse.

Susan at the Party

Susan sits alone in her room.

Clean Discomfort: She is aware of feelings of loneliness, sadness, and anxiety swirling within her emotional experience. There are thoughts present regarding missed social opportunities for the evening and mental noise popping into her head describing a socially desolate future.

Dirty Discomfort: Her reaction to the clean discomfort includes tightening her muscles against the discomfort, pacing her small room, and breathing shallowly. She is latching onto the following thoughts.

- "Wow, I am a weak, crazy loser for feeling this way."
- "I need to snap out of this right now!"
- "Ugh! Why am I still feeling this way?"
- "Oh God, I can't stand this!"
- "No one else feels this way; I am hopeless."

Suddenly, Susan's phone dings. She has gotten a text from a classmate inviting her to a party this evening.

Clean Discomfort: She becomes aware of a swirl of anticipatory anxiety and automatic thoughts and images of rejection and social maladjustment.

Dirty Discomfort: She further tightens her muscles in response to the anxiety. She grits her teeth and balls her hands up into fists. She latches onto the following thoughts.

- "I cannot go out feeling this way."
- "What the hell is wrong with me?"
- "I just need to relax so that I can go out. Okay, one, two, three ... RELAX, DAMN IT!"
- "Oh, God, it's not working!"
- "C'mon, you stupid loser, relax for once in your life ... RELAX!"
- "It's getting worse. I can't stand it!"

After forty-five minutes of this, she struggles out the door and somehow manages to force herself to go to the party. She walks in alone and begins to scour the party for people she knows.

Clean Discomfort: She is aware of the feelings of awkwardness and anxiety of being in a room full of strangers. She is aware of lots of automatic brain chatter about rejection and not fitting in.

Dirty Discomfort: She is tightening the muscles in her body to a painful degree. She is holding her breath and desperately struggling to relax. She fuses with the following thoughts.

- "I shouldn't be feeling this."

- "No one else here feels anxious and awkward. I am such a loser!"
- "I just need to relax, then I can talk to people ... RELAX, DAMN IT!"
- "It's not working. Try harder!"
- "I can't take this. This is supposed to be fun."
- "I gotta get the hell out of here. This is too uncomfortable!"

After five minutes of inner turmoil, Susan flees the party and rushes back to her dorm room to hide. She falls upon her bed feeling defeated and hopeless.

Susan's Cup of Discomfort

DIRTY DISCOMFORT

- Tightening the muscles in her body to a painful degree
- Holding her breath and desperately struggling to relax
- Fusing with the following thoughts:
  "I shouldn't be feeling this!"
  "No one else here feels anxious and awkward! I am such a loser!"
  "I just need to relax, then I can talk to people ... RELAX DAMN IT!"
  "It's not working ... try harder!"
  "I can't take this! This is supposed to be fun!"
  "I gotta get the hell out of here! This is too uncomfortable!"

CLEAN DISCOMFORT

- Awareness of thoughts and images of rejection
- Awareness of anxious feelings
- Baseline self-consciousness or perceptions of awkwardness

Notice the amount of dirty discomfort that is layered onto Susan's clean discomfort. The clean discomfort is unpleasant, but far more tolerable than the total discomfort that comes with the addition of the dirty discomfort. Susan's life would be easier in the moment if she were able to minimize the additional self-imposed discomfort.

EXERCISE: What's in your cup?

Select an activity that triggers a moderate amount of social anxiety. Activity:

Engage in that activity and stay long enough in order to observe both your clean discomfort and your dirty discomfort. Write them on your cup.

If you have difficulty with identifying your dirty discomfort, then ask yourself in the moment, "What am I doing to try to feel better?" and "How am I trying to push away or fight against the anxiety either physically or mentally?" Additionally, ask yourself, "How am I blaming or reprimanding myself for feeling this way? How much am I fusing with those thoughts?"

Remember, the clean discomfort is the automatic anxious reaction to the situation that you are aware of without any resistance or judgment.

My Cup of Discomfort

Were you surprised at the amount of dirty discomfort?

THE UNCOMFORTABLE REALITY OF SOCIAL DISCOMFORT

Clean social discomfort is unavoidable for most of us in at least some social situations—at least to some degree. Dirty discomfort happens to most of us at least some of the time and can greatly increase total discomfort in a given social situation (or the anticipation of a social situation). Despite the promise of "cures" from various books and a rogues gallery of gurus, the reality of social discomfort persists. You can, however, work to lessen, manage, cope and even thrive in the face of social discomfort, both dirty and clean.

DEALING WITH DIRTY DISCOMFORT

Dirty Discomfort: We all do it sometimes!

I feel ill at this moment. That is my clean discomfort. At times, however, I am catching myself tighten against the physical discomfort. My teeth just now are gritted together in resistance to the sinus pressure. I am aware that my shoulders are hunched and my stomach is tense. I also notice that I am fusing with the thought, "I shouldn't have to be sick right now!" My tension signifies that I have been pouring dirty discomfort onto the clean.

Now that I have become aware of this dirty discomfort, however, I can let go. I can let my jaw loosen, soften around my shoulders and stomach, and let go of the thoughts. I can surrender my resistance to the clean discomfort. Now, my sense of suffering in the face of unpleasant physical sensations has eased and I am ready to move forward with the task at hand.

Imagine that you are in a triggering social situation and your cup is overflowing with social discomfort. Let's also imagine that you have decided that you are not going to take the easy or quick way out of this by fleeing the situation or using a substance to numb out. You have decided that now is a time to move forward in a socially courageous way and take steps toward accomplishing social goals. You've decided that in this moment you are not going to allow anxiety to control you.

First of all—good for the imaginary you! Now, let's see how you can keep moving forward while minimizing your dirty discomfort and sense of suffering.

Prerequisites

Prerequisites are those things that you need to have prior to achieving a particular goal. For example, you must take the Introduction to Psychology course before taking the Advanced Psychotherapies course. In order to minimize your dirty discomfort, you need to have the following prerequisites.

1. Willingness to accept the reality of having a noisy brain.
2. Willingness to live with a reasonable amount of social uncertainty.
3. Willingness to be human and, therefore, be socially imperfect.

If you have at least some amount of those prerequisites, let's proceed.

When you enter a social situation, take the following steps.

Step 1: Disengage your autopilot as much as possible

When something makes you feel socially uncomfortable, the normal instinct is to avoid it or use safety behaviors, which then digs you deeper into the social anxiety hole. The goal of Step 1 is to begin paying attention to how you automatically react to anxiety so that you can stop yourself from mindlessly doing what anxiety tells you to do.

When you are feeling uncomfortable, let that be the cue to check in with your experience. Make up your mind that you (and not anxiety) will decide how you respond to your social discomfort.

Step 2: See the value of no self-judgment and choose self-compassion instead

One of the keys to minimizing dirty social discomfort is, ironically, accepting and normalizing the clean discomfort. Rather than condemning yourself for what your brain and body are automatically doing, see it as normal for you at that point in time in that particular context. Rather than calling yourself "weak" (or latching onto a similar automatic thought), allow it to be what it is—brain noise and bodily sensations—and let yourself know that it truly is okay for that experience, in that moment, to be there. You are part of the human species and social discomfort is normal for most of us. Hold yourself with compassion (and the same for the human species) as you allow yourself to coexist with your experience.

Step 3: Do a brief body scan and lower your resistance

When you experience the clean social discomfort, take a moment and notice where in your body you are resisting (tightening against) the discomfort. Then focus on easing that struggle. Soften your resistance by softening the muscles in and around those body parts. If you are like most of my clients and workshop participants, you will immediately think that this is supposed to be a relaxation exercise. It is not.

In fact, trying to relax when feeling highly anxious can become an emotional avoidance strategy that may backfire and actually increase your anxiety. If you fuse with the thought that you "MUST relax or else!", you are likely throwing gasoline on the anxiety fire. Fighting to relax is like fighting to fall asleep—it is the opposite of helpful.

Instead, you are trying to surrender any resistance to the social anxiety that you are naturally experiencing. Rather than trying to relax, you are trying to ease your fight against the anxiety and make a soft space for it to be there. It is like gently holding a crying baby rather than screaming at it to quiet down. Or, it is like being a ragdoll riding a rollercoaster—you soften and flow along with the social discomfort ride.

A mindful body scan entails paying attention to each muscle group, observing (without judgment) where there is tightening against clean discomfort and surrendering that struggle as much as you can, while accepting whatever you cannot initially let go of.

There are many variations on this ancient exercise. Here is one.

EXERCISE: Mindful Body Scan

When you are aware of a high level of social discomfort, try this:

Briefly and without judgment, notice:

… your toes, bottoms of your feet, tops of your feet, and heels. On a scale of one to ten, see how much resistance to the anxiety you are experiencing in the form of tightening, fidgeting, or the urge to tense in and around your feet. Observe how much of this struggle you can let go of. Make the softest space you can for the clean anxiety to coexist with you. Do not try to make the anxiety go away right now. Let it be.

… your calves, shins, around your knees, your upper legs, and hips. On a scale of one to ten, see how much resistance to the anxiety you are experiencing in the form of tightening, fidgeting, or the urge to tense in and around your legs. Observe how much of this struggle you can let go of. Make the softest space you can for the clean anxiety to coexist with you. Do not try to make the anxiety go away right now. Allow the anxiety to softly flow as it is.

... your hips, stomach, and lower back. On a scale of one to ten, see how much resistance to the anxiety you are experiencing in the form of tightening, fidgeting, or the urge to tense in and around these muscle groups. Make the softest space you can for the clean discomfort to coexist with you. Let go of the fight. Let go of the struggle.

... your fingers, palms of your hands, backs of your hands, and wrists. On a scale of one to ten, see how much resistance to the anxiety you are experiencing in the form of tightening, fidgeting, or the urge to tense in and around your hands and wrists. Make the softest space you can for the clean discomfort to coexist with you. Let it be there, softly and with your permission.

... your forearms, upper arms, biceps and triceps, and shoulders. On a scale of one to ten, see how much resistance to the anxiety you are experiencing in the form of tightening, fidgeting, or the urge to tense in and around your arms. Soften and surrender the fight. Allow yourself to feel what you feel without resistance. Let it go.

... your chest, upper back, and in and around your shoulder blades. On a scale of one to ten, see how much resistance to the anxiety you are experiencing in the form of tightening, fidgeting, or the urge to tense in and around your upper body. Make the softest space you can for the clean anxiety to coexist with you. Let go of the struggle to change your emotions. Let them just be as they are, without judgment or resistance.

... your neck, jaw, lips, cheeks, and around your eyes, forehead, and scalp. On a scale of one to ten, see how much resistance to the anxiety you are experiencing in the form of tightening, fidgeting, or the urge to tense in and around your face and head. Let go of as much struggle against the clean discomfort as you can. Soften into the discomfort and let go of the fight to change it. Let it be.

Now briefly scan your entire body from toes on up to your forehead, looking for additional resistance to the discomfort and see if you can let go of any more of the struggle, even a little bit.

TIPS:

- Check in with your breathing regularly. If you are holding your breath or breathing shallowly, you are likely fighting the clean discomfort. Allow your breathing to be as normal as possible. If you are tightening your stomach or chest, odds are you are altering your breathing in an unhelpful way.

- The body scan can go on for as long as you want or as short as you need. You can focus on every tiny muscle group or you can check in with:
    - Lower body
    - Upper body
    - Head
    - Or simply, Entire Body (1-2 seconds).

- If you have practiced this and realize that you mostly struggle with one or two body parts (for example, gritting your teeth and tightening your stomach), then you can focus on those parts only.

- When you're in the social situation, I would encourage you to periodically do a brief body scan and practice releasing the struggle whenever you become aware of it.

- This exercise can be practiced alone for a longer experience (like a meditation) if you would like. However, you can use this coping tool when you are in the socially uncomfortable situation itself (rather than escaping the situation in order to use it).

- Don't spend too much time in your head doing this. Quickly scanning for dirty discomfort, softening, and then refocusing externally on the social task at hand is the key.

- If you use this acceptance-based exercise as a way to make the clean social discomfort go away, you run the risk of adding even more dirty social discomfort. The goal is to more peacefully coexist with clean social discomfort, not to remove it.

- Remember that this is just one strategy. If you find it unhelpful after practicing, don't beat yourself up. Use a different tool. However, in my experience, this is a very useful tool for most people.

Step 4: Use defusion strategies

Defusion strategies, such as the ones you learned to use for social anxiety thoughts, can also be used for coping with anxious feelings and reducing dirty discomfort.

Here are some examples.

Be the observer, not the sensation

Rather than fusing with the anxious feelings, observe them like you are an anthropologist observing a native tribe from a distance.

Fusing with the Anxiety	Observing the Anxiety
I can't stand this.	I am aware of sweaty palms and an urge to leave.
This better go away!	I am noticing my fight-or-flight response being triggered.
Why do I have to feel this way?	There are anxious feelings present and an urge to tighten my muscles to resist them.

Predict and then welcome anxiety

If you know that you typically feel anxious in a given social situation, expect it rather than wish it not to be there. Then when you enter the situation and the anxious feelings arise, welcome them. Acknowledge, "There you are, my friend," and allow them to play in the background while you refocus on the social task at hand.

Pretend there is a big prize!

If by sitting with this feeling for the duration of the social event you would be guaranteed to win a three-hundred-million-dollar mega lottery jackpot, you might choose to sit with this feeling differently. Rather than fusing with the thought that you have to get rid of the anxiety right this moment, you might eagerly and gently hold the emotion in higher regard. You would likely soften into and coexist with the clean discomfort, which would then lead to a decrease in your dirty discomfort.

Try pretending that rather than the anxiety being a problem that needs to be eradicated, it is a ticket to winning a big prize. If social anxiety has been holding you back from achieving valued social goals such as friendship, romance, and career advancement, then learning to more peacefully coexist may in fact lead to an actual valuable prize.

Find your emotional reaction fascinating

"Isn't it interesting that my body is experiencing an evolutionary reaction designed to keep me alive in the face of hostile tribes and ferocious sabertooth tigers when I want to stop by and say hello to Sue from Accounting?"

"Wow, I'm on a date with Stan and my body is reacting as if I am bungee jumping off the Eiffel Tower."

Channel your inner warrior: Demand more anxiety

When you experience socially anxious feelings and feel the urge to struggle to get rid of them, which most likely will make them stronger, you can try the opposite—demand more! The more you are truly willing to courageously coexist with greater amounts of clean social anxiety, the less dirty social anxiety you are likely to have.

When you notice the presence of clean anxiety, imagine your favorite tough action hero staring the anxiety in the eye and calmly asking, "Is that the best you've got?" You might find that the dirty discomfort shrinks in the face of such bold acceptance. You can also remind yourself that over time you can build up a greater anxiety tolerance and at the same time learn that you can experience social discomfort without a catastrophic outcome.

Step 5: Keep moving forward

Keep your eye on the prize and continue put one foot in front of the other—moving ever forward toward your social goals.

Dirty discomfort: The bottom line

The more unwilling you are to experience the clean social discomfort—the more you demonize it, hate it, fight it, and the more you castigate yourself for experiencing it—the more dirty discomfort (and suffering) you are likely to experience. Genuine and nonjudgmental willingness is ultimately the best antidote to the heaping portions of dirty discomfort we humans often layer onto our daily clean discomfort.

MINIMIZING THE PRESENCE OF CLEAN SOCIAL DISCOMFORT

Stanley

Stanley was burning the candle at both ends. He had a big presentation to give at work first thing in the morning and it was already midnight and he was just sitting down to prepare it. He could imagine no terror worse than having to get up in front of his boss and coworkers and give a fifteen-minute talk on the relative merits of upgrading their internet security technology—a subject he was asked to look into, but he knew nothing about. He hated public speaking and hadn't wanted to even think about his upcoming presentation. So, he procrastinated until the last possible moment and now he had no choice but to stay up all night researching the topic and preparing his presentation.

However, he was fully stocked up with two large take-out cups of black coffee and a jumbo bag of cheesy puffs. He was ready to get in the zone and prepare a phenomenal presentation ... just a quick check of his email to get warmed up. Four hours and five Netflix shows later, panic sets in. He knew he wouldn't be ready. *He was a dead man walking!*

Cliché of the day

Clean social discomfort is going to remain a fact of life for most people in at least some situations. So how do you cope in the face of this reality? It comes down to the old acceptance prayer, loosely paraphrased as, change what you can and accept what you cannot. Cliché, yes, but so relevant. You can work to reduce clean social discomfort by making specific changes in your life.

The types of changes you can make in order to reduce clean discomfort are not immediate quick fixes such as avoiding or fleeing the situation (or emotionally numbing out to the situation via mind-altering substances). Changing your anxiety by way of avoidances will prevent you from learning that you can handle the situation and may consequently lead you away from your long-term social goals while actually ramping up your clean discomfort the next time you are in those situations.

It is best to decide which changes are both effective *and* in your best long-term interest—rather than as a momentary impulse.

EXERCISE: It's time to play Accept or Change!

Which of these items below do you think are worthy of your investment of time and emotional energy to try to change? Which ones are better off accepted?

Place a **C** if you think it is worthwhile to try to change or **A** if it is better to accept, make the best of it, and move forward with your life:

- ☐ I have no friends
- ☐ I have a naturally shy temperament
- ☐ I am out of shape
- ☐ If I move toward my social goals, I might get rejected at some point
- ☐ I am in an abusive relationship

☐ First dates are awkward at times
☐ I avoid uncomfortable social situations
☐ I am imperfect socially
☐ I sometimes experience social anxiety

The goal of this exercise is not to tell you what to do or not do. It is to help you begin to look at what you have control over and then YOU can choose what to try to change or not.

If you have no friends, you can make changes in your life that will increase the likelihood of making some, whether by joining a social group or learning and practicing new social skills. On the other hand, having a shy temperament is your birthright. You can choose to embrace this reality and live the best shy-tempered life you can, but there are no changes that you could make to transform yourself into a gregarious extrovert.

If you are out of shape and want to improve your conditioning, you can make lifestyle changes such as joining a gym or arranging to walk a few days a week with your neighbor, Beatrice. You cannot, however, change the reality that if you choose to interact with fellow members of the human species, rejection will likely occur at times—though you can observe that rejection is infrequent and not catastrophic.

If you are in an abusive relationship, you can take steps to change that situation, though it may be difficult and risky.

You cannot change the reality that there is inherent awkwardness (for most of us) at times during a first date. You can, however, choose to try to view your first date awkwardness with a sense of humor.

You can choose to change an unhealthy pattern of avoiding uncomfortable social situations (given the high personal cost that comes with such avoidance). On the other hand, no matter how much you hope, wish, and try to become socially perfect, it is an endeavor destined for failure. The best you can do is try your best while accepting and embracing the limitations of being human.

Should you try to change the fact that sometimes you experience social anxiety? Given that social anxiety is a normal part of life, if you choose to be part of a human society, you are better off accepting the experience of social anxiety. You can, however, minimize your dirty discomfort while choosing to take steps to reduce the clean discomfort as well; you just cannot eradicate it altogether.

Having a nervous system that is anxious or stressed in general will likely increase your clean social discomfort in your triggering situations. Below are some ways to reduce your general arousal level so that you are less amped up in social situations. These approaches are designed to reduce clean discomfort.

Minimize caffeine

I will admit it: I love caffeine. Coffee is my favorite beverage. It is, however, a very reliable producer of clean anxiety—it wakes up the nervous system. It gives me the energy to teach evening classes or go for a morning jog around the neighborhood. However, if you are already doing something anxiety-provoking, you can minimize additional clean anxiety by minimizing caffeine intake.

Have reasonably healthy nutritional practices

Diets high in simple carbohydrates (such as sweets, white bread, or chips of all kinds) can lead to dramatic fluctuations in blood sugar. Blood sugar drops can increase baseline anxiety. Also, going long periods of time without eating can cause an increase in clean anxiety as your blood sugar dips.

Exercise regularly

Regular exercise can reduce anxiety. This is especially true of cardiovascular exercise (walking, running, tennis, and so forth) but being physically active in general, no matter the exercise type, is helpful.

Practice general stress management

If you are going to be facing a social-anxiety-triggering situation (such as a first date) AND you are stressed out in general, your level of clean anxiety will be higher. If you have good stress management practices, your clean anxiety will likely be less right from the start.

Examples of good stress management practices include:

- *What a loser!*
- *You'll make a fool out of yourself.*
- *She probably won't show up and you'll be humiliated.*

Susan instinctively began to repeat her pattern of struggle, and the dirty pain began to rise. She became aware of her body tightening and her breath constricting. She also became aware of a strong urge to text her acquaintance and cancel, then flee back to the privacy of her room as she had done countless times before.

No, this time she was determined to break that pattern. She scanned her body and gently softened her clenched stomach and jaw muscles. She reminded herself of her goals of making closer friendships and developing a romantic relationship. She told herself that she would gladly pay the price of having this clean discomfort if it means moving toward her goals. She slowly settled into the moment, holding her pain gently, like a crying baby, and soon the urgency left. She smiled inwardly and mentally patted herself on the back. "You've got this," she told herself compassionately.

This is when her new life began.

Leaving Your Social Comfort Zone

Disregarding the siren call of avoidance

Gus

Gus sticks to his friend, Sid, with desperate insecurity. Sid is the golden child and darling of Eastside High. Sid radiates a sparkling mix of social, athletic, and intellectual superiority, whereas Gus feels strikingly bereft of any of these attributes. Despite his portrayal as Sid's confident sidekick, on the inside he feels self-conscious around his friend and others his age, always fearful they will take notice of his anxious awkwardness and condemn him for it.

Yet Gus continues to be Sid's closest friend. He tries to feel content basking (or rather hiding) in Sid's shadow, ever afraid to branch out on his own. But when the inevitable spotlight happens to shine in his direction, he quickly flees back into the semi-comfort of Sid's glow—redirecting the spotlight to his friend, where he feels it belongs.

Gus's life revolves around his friend and his friend's interests, challenges, and accomplishments, which, of course, suits Sid just fine. After all, Sid was born to bask in the attention of others and he relishes Gus's attention.

For the past few years, Gus has had a crush on his classmate, Simone. He thought and wished that perhaps she liked him as well. However, he had remained terrified to ask her out on a date and, to his dismay, Sid recently swept in and invited her to the prom. Gus was the first to high-five Sid's good fortune when she agreed to go with him, and he even agreed to be their designated driver since he is nothing if not loyal.

While Gus has his own dreams and ambitions, he keeps those tucked deep inside, never daring to expose them to the light. Other students find Gus to have a quiet charm, but Gus is afraid to stray from his predictable and safe friendship with Sid and venture out into the broader social world.

Increasingly, Gus is feeling painfully lonely, socially frightened, and deeply self-doubting. Will he ever have a life of his own or is he destined to live the rest of his life hiding glumly in Sid's vast shadow?

THE COURAGE TO CHANGE

We've discussed (and hopefully you've practiced) coping and thriving in the presence of socially anxious thoughts and emotions. Now it is time to take the show on the road and begin to seek out socially challenging situations in order to practice using these skills in the real world of social discomfort.

The Benefits of Leaving Your Social Comfort Zones

Entering social situations that are comfortable and familiar may be pleasant, but it is not socially courageous. This is okay if you are able to get your social needs met within your comfort zone. However, having the social courage to venture beyond what is comfortable can broaden your social comfort zones and can lead to benefits.

1. If you put a social fear to the test and learn that the feared outcome does not occur, then you'll likely have less discomfort in that situation in the future.

2. Increasing your willingness to experience the natural and universal experience of social anxiety, rather than resisting it, can build up your social-anxiety-tolerance muscles. Over time, the same level of social discomfort may feel less unpleasant to experience.

3. Repeatedly challenging yourself by entering uncomfortable social situations gives you the opportunity to learn and practice new social skills or brush up on old ones.

4. Practicing approaching uncomfortable social situations rather than automatically defaulting to avoidance can lead you to feel like you are more in control of your social goals—allowing you to move forward toward these goals one step at a time.

Experience Is the Best Teacher

As we discussed earlier in the book, it is not social situations that cause high levels of anxiety, it is how you interpret those situations. If your belief is that you will get harshly rejected and will be unable to cope in a particular circumstance, then a high level of social anxiety is reasonable.

One approach is to look at the evidence for and against the belief that the situation is socially "dangerous" like we discussed in the section on beliefs. Nothing, however, can help you modify a belief as effectively as your own experience. If you believe that if you interact with a poodle that you will get ferociously mauled, it may help somewhat to look at the statistics on poodle-related attacks, but spending a few hours hanging out with Fluffy will allow you to learn through your own experience that not all poodles will harm you.

In this way you become a scientist conducting an experiment:

Theory A: Fluffy will attack if I spend an hour alone in the room with her.

Theory B: I will be safe spending an hour alone with Fluffy.

After spending the hour alone with Fluffy, you will learn whether theory A or B is correct. If B is correct, then you are free to experiment with more dogs in different settings and will probably have less fear in the future. If theory A is correct then you can learn to become more discerning of the type of dog you associate with or learn and practice new skills for interacting with dogs more effectively so that you have a more positive outcome in the future.

Similarly, you can experiment with humans as well.

Behavioral Experiments: Studying Your Fellow Humans

I've always admired the adventurous curiosity of anthropologists. They can be found studying humans in the most remote parts of the world, interacting with indigenous tribes, taking part in their customs, and all the while using keen observations skills to take in the complexities of their behaviors and rituals. This type of active observation is often in sharp contrast to the behavior of people suffering from high levels of social discomfort or worry.

Instead of taking part in native social customs with sharply focused observation, people with high levels of social anxiety often remain focused inward during the social gatherings and rituals of their local tribe. As a result of their self-directed focus, they may miss out on connecting with others on a deeper level. They typically overlook the nuances of people's actual reactions to them while imagining negative reactions are occurring through the filter of their internal focus.

For example, if you give a talk in front of an audience and stare at your notecards throughout, you miss out on your audience's reaction to your talk. At the same time, you may be imagining that they are hostile, looking bored, or getting up and walking out with bewildered looks on their faces. If you don't direct your attention externally—to your audience—then at the end of your talk, you are left to analyze your imagined audience reactions when deciding how well your talk went. You would then be analyzing bad data. Additionally, your lack of external focus on your audience will likely lead to less of a connection with them and thus diminish your performance.

This internal focus for some of us can be a long-standing and persistent habit. Perhaps you have habitually avoided eye contact for many years, or been more focused in social situations on what to say next rather than what your conversation partner is saying now. It might be that you have drawn conclusions about other humans following many years' worth of inaccurate data. Isn't it interesting to think that perhaps the way you believe other people react to you might (at least to some degree) be heavily skewed by your inner fears rather than the external reality?

Marina

The fact that Marina's face flushed bright red when she was feeling socially anxious was a never-ending source of personal turmoil for her. She went to great lengths to avoid the utter humiliation of having other people witness her face's outward betrayal of her inner feelings. Blushing was not only her Slavic heritage—it was her own personal shame.

Her belief was that blushing would lead to public humiliation and she didn't feel she could tolerate other people's rejecting glances and cruel comments. As a result, her social life was loaded with avoidance along with a hearty slathering of makeup and worry. When blushing, she avoided looking at other people and retreated to the confines of her mind where she imagined exaggerated shades of red and cruel responses to her enhanced facial color.

She never really questioned whether her fears were valid or whether they were simply the result of an active and imaginative noisy brain.

That's not to say that everyone will treat us well in life if we just pay attention. No one receives universal approval and there is no escaping the fact that some people will bark and some will bite. However, if you are more sucked up into your head rather than focused outwardly on others, you may not have an accurate sense for how people are reacting to you. For the most part, people with high levels of social anxiety tend to think people are more rejecting than they actually are.

It is now time to put your scientist hat on and go out into the world of humans and conduct some research. When you venture into uncomfortable or uncharted social territory you may notice a couple of competing theories regarding how the people you encounter will react to you.

Anxiety's Theory:	Social situation X is exceedingly risky and if I get rejected, it will be unbearable.
Competing Theory:	I am unlikely to get rejected in social situation X, and even if I do, it won't be nearly as traumatic as I imagine.

Remember, it is not just the social situation that people fear, but what happens in that social situation. For example, going to a party may be okay, but significant fear increases with the worry of blushing, sweating, or making a social mistake while at the party. Therefore, it is not necessarily enough to test your experience with the situation itself (though that is a fantastic start). You must see what happens if you blush, sweat, or make a social mistake—IF that is what you fear.

To do this, you can intentionally blush (accomplished by eating spicy food, thinking naughty thoughts, or pinching your cheeks), for example, and then direct your focus externally to see how the people you interact with react. By intentionally causing the "problem" you are worried about, you have the opportunity to observe what really happens.

Of course, there are certain antisocial behaviors guaranteed to cause intense societal rejection and even get you thrown in jail—so use the following rule of thumb when deciding upon a social challenge experiment. Ask yourself, does this situation happen to people some of the time without a catastrophic outcome? It is normal to blush, sweat, forget someone's name, stumble over your words or feet, have a minor wardrobe malfunction, forget to brush your hair, and so on. Everyone misspeaks, makes mistakes, and wedges their foot in their mouth every once in a while.

Gus

Here are some of the theories Gus's anxiety has about him.

- If Gus goes to a party without Sid, no one will want to talk to him.

- If Gus raises his hand to answer a question in class, he will give the wrong answer and everyone will make fun of him. He will become a laughing stock at his school.
- If Gus gives a presentation in class, he will become paralyzed with fear and be unable to continue. Everyone will laugh.
- If Gus tells Sid that he will be unable to be the driver for prom, Sid will be angry and their friendship will end.
- If Gus stumbles awkwardly while walking down the main school corridor, everyone will laugh at him and talk about it for weeks to come.
- If Gus's hand trembles slightly while talking to Simone, then she will notice and harshly belittle him for it.

EXERCISE: What are anxiety's theories that cause you added social discomfort?

....

....

....

....

....

....

....

....

....

....

....

....

....

....

....

Set Your Pace

Now is the time to begin moving into socially uncomfortable situations (at your pace … no one else's!) with your eyes and mind both open to what really occurs, rather than what you imagine. The nice thing about social anxiety fears is that you typically don't need to go far in order to challenge yourself—people are everywhere!

First, decide how much time and energy you are willing to put into social experimentation. It is your life and your decision how to prioritize your time. If you just want to slightly "dip your toes in the water" for now, that is okay. If you want to take a few months and make it your number-one priority, that's good, too. You set your pace—and should you wake up tomorrow and wish to shift gears, by all means go for it.

I suggest you approach your social experimentation with a plan rather than half-heartedly. If it is a slow pace you wish to start with, embrace that pace rather than beating yourself up for going slowly. If you choose a plan that is more intense, give yourself permission to make that time a priority, even if it means putting some other goals, temporarily, on the backburner.

MY INITIAL PACE (check one):

- ☐ Slow, test-the-waters pace (One challenge each week)
- ☐ Slow-but-steady pace (Two to three challenges each week)
- ☐ Moderate pace (Four to five challenges each week)
- ☐ Quick pace (Six challenges each week)
- ☐ Very quick pace (At least one challenge per day—every day!)

If you set a slow pace and then get concerned that your progress is also slow, rather than giving up, consider upping your pace. If you are feeling overly stressed out because of the high intensity level of your pace, then you could either try to stick it out or slow your pace. Beware of the all-or-nothing or perfectionistic thinking patterns that anxiety may toss your way.

Testing Anxiety's Theories

Choose one of anxiety's theories and come up with a method to test it out. Perhaps you worry about looking nervous. Specify the way you fear looking nervous (I'll shake, blush, sweat, fidget, voice will crack, and so on). Come up with a plan to simulate that concern.

For example:

- I will jog to the party to show up sweaty.
- I will pinch my cheeks until they appear flushed before the business meeting.
- I will order a cookie at the bakery and when it is handed to me, change my mind and ask for a muffin instead.
- I will make my hands slightly tremble when talking to my classmates at a party.

The range of experiments is infinite and should be tailored to your particular social concerns. Here are more examples of situations you can make the center of experiments.

- Make eye contact with five strangers in passing
- Mess up your hair and walk in public for ten minutes
- Smile at five strangers in passing
- Go to a clothing store and try on clothing, but do not buy
- Say "hello" to five strangers in passing
- Give a compliment to a friend, store or restaurant employee, or stranger
- Half tuck/un-tuck your shirt in public for ten minutes
- Ask a salesperson for help finding an item
- Call a business and make an appointment, then call back five minutes later and cancel it
- Walk in front of others
- Talk loudly on your cell phone in front of strangers
- Select the restaurant or type of food for a group outing
- Make an intentional mistake while talking to a friend, clerk, or stranger

- Self-disclose something personal to a friend
- Have a conversation with a stranger with a five second awkward silence
- Go for a walk and bump into someone
- Eat out alone at a restaurant
- Initiate a conversation with a stranger
- Eat or drink awkwardly in front of a friend or stranger
- Find an excuse to ask an authority figure a question (police, boss, principal or dean of school)
- Ask a friend a personal question
- Ask a stranger to recommend a store or restaurant
- Leave a goofy name when the coffee shop clerk asks for your name
- Interrupt someone while they're talking
- Take a dollar into a store and ask an employee for change
- Ask someone an obvious question (For example, at a burger restaurant, inquire, "Do you have burgers?")
- Drop silverware while eating around friends or strangers
- Purposely trip in front of friends or strangers
- Ask to sit with or next to someone at a cafeteria or bar
- Roll one sleeve up and one down for ten minutes and ask a store clerk a question during that time
- Initiate a conversation with an attractive person
- Select a seat in a crowded room that feels out in the open
- "Fumble for money" for sixty seconds when purchasing an item
- Sit on a bench for five minutes and say hello to everyone who passes by
- While in your car, turn on the radio and sing out loud to songs you know, particularly when you are stopped at a traffic light and there are cars beside you
- Spill some of your drink while socializing
- Make loud noise (for example, cough, sneeze, or squeak your chair) in a quiet store, restaurant, or coffee shop
- Call about a bulletin board posting

- Answer a question incorrectly
- Start to ask someone a question and "forget" the question—don't apologize
- Purposefully stutter when talking
- Purposefully mispronounce a word during a conversation
- Ask a local business if they are hiring
- Interrupt a busy salesperson
- Engage a salesperson in conversation and walk away without buying anything ("waste their time")
- Wait in line to buy something, say you forgot an item, then go back through the same line
- Ask an obvious question to a stranger or friend (Where is store X when you are standing next to it)
- Ask for a job application at a store
- Ask an employee at a store how they like working there
- Use the stall or urinal in a public bathroom next to someone
- At a bookstore, buy and return a book just after five minutes, ask for your money back because you "changed your mind"
- Wear your shirt inside out or backwards in a public place for ten minutes
- Walk around in public with toilet paper stuck to your shoe as if you didn't know it was there
- Ask a bookstore employee about a children's book and involve him in a conversation—find out if the clerk has any children of his own, and if so, how old they are
- Intentionally mispronounce a salesperson's name (if they have a name badge)
- Go to a jewelry store and ask if they sell keys
- Request to taste three different ice cream flavors at an ice cream shop
- At a bookstore, take a book off the shelf and recite several sentences out loud from where you are standing
- Choose something you enjoyed while you were at a restaurant and find a waiter, manager, chef, or owner and convey your compliments to them

- Ask a stranger for directions
- Put a loud, attention-getting ringtone on your phone, then have someone call you when you're in a crowded but quiet store
- Call three numbers from the phonebook, and when someone answers, ask to speak with Mrs. Franklin. If you are told there is no Mrs. Franklin or that you have the wrong number, say "I'm sorry" and hang up
- Smile, establish two seconds of eye contact and say "hello" to a stranger—then repeat five times with different people
- When driving, wave at a stranger like you know them (it only counts if they see you)
- Ride an elevator with a stranger and stand a bit too close

If you have a friend or family member who would like to be less controlled by social anxiety, then you could partner up with them. You do an experiment and they observe the outcome and then vice versa. This can be helpful for bolstering motivation and for having an additional person to observe people's reactions during the experiment.

Conduct the social experiment with open eyes and open mind

You are now a social scientist. Your objective is to determine how people genuinely respond to you and to your perceived physical or behavioral "flaws." Did you get rejected? Was it catastrophic? Were the thoughts and emotions that you experienced so horrendous that you must give up on your social goals? Or were they merely clean discomfort that you could invite along and willingly accept?

On the Behavioral Experiment form, you will design and carry out a social experiment based on testing anxiety's theory that catastrophic rejection will occur if you do or do not do certain things (attend a social function, talk to a new person, appear anxious, and so forth).

First, you will record the specific experiment that you plan to undertake. These experiments need to be specific and within your control. For example, saying, "I'll challenge myself at a party" is too vague. Stating, "I'll introduce myself to three people" is specific. Saying, "I'll go on a date" is not necessarily in your control. Saying, "I'll ask Bobbie to meet for coffee" is within your control.

Once you have written down the specific experiment, jot down the outcome that anxiety predicts will happen. Again, this must be concrete and observable. For example, "They will laugh at me, they will yell at me, they will walk away and not respond to me … " and so on.

Then, go and do the experiment. Keep in mind that it is of utmost importance that you pay attention externally to what happens so that you collect valid data on people's actual response versus your imagined version of their response. Try to use only descriptive language when recording what actually happened, rather than evaluative language based on tricks like mind reading or jumping to conclusions based on a feeling.

Examples of Evaluative Language	Examples of Descriptive Language
He thought I was weird	She smiled
She did not like me	He maintained eye contact
I made them uncomfortable	They nodded their heads as I spoke
It went terribly	She talked with me for five minutes
I really messed things up	No one laughed at me
They did not want me there	No one approached me

Gus's Social Experiments

Experiment 1: Go to a party without Sid.

- **Predicted Outcome:** No one will talk to me.
- **Actual Outcome:** Several people greeted me when I entered. I had three conversations lasting more than five minutes each. People made eye contact and smiled. A cute girl complimented me on my Pink Floyd T-shirt.
- **Reasonable Conclusion:** People seemed friendly and although I was nervous, no one seemed to know or care.

Experiment 2: Raise my hand to answer a question during geometry class.

- **Predicted Outcome:** I'll get the answer wrong and everyone will laugh at me. Then it'll get around the whole school.
- **Actual Outcome:** I did it twice. The first time I got it right, though I did not observe any students looking in my direction or changing their behavior in any way. The second time I intentionally gave the wrong answer. No one laughed and actually they appeared to behave the same as when I got the answer right.
- **Reasonable Conclusion:** People seem into their own heads and lives. My answers in class don't seem to be a big deal either way.

Experiment 3: Give a presentation in history class

- **Predicted Outcome:** I'll be so nervous that I will freeze up and won't be able to finish the presentation. People will make fun of me for it.
- **Actual Outcome:** I was very nervous, but did not freeze up. I worried that people could see that I was nervous, but no one laughed or appeared to notice. I got an A on the presentation and one guy even said, "Good job."
- **Reasonable Conclusion:** Although uncomfortable, it went okay. I coped reasonably well with the discomfort. People did not appear eager to reject me.

Experiment 4: Tell Sid that I won't be able to drive him and Simone around on prom night.

- **Predicted Outcome:** Sid will get angry and our friendship will end.
- **Actual Outcome:** He said he thought I was kidding about driving and had already made arrangements for a limousine to drive them. He asked if I wanted to ride with them in the limo.

- **Reasonable Conclusion:** Maybe my friendship is not so fragile.

Experiment 5: Stumble noticeably while walking in the crowded hallway between classes.

- **Predicted Outcome:** Everyone will laugh and make fun of me for weeks to come.
- **Actual Outcome:** I did it three times. No one looked or appeared to notice.
- **Reasonable Conclusion:** Maybe the spotlight on me is only in my mind.

What I am learning from these experiments: It does not appear that people are ready to attack or humiliate me if I make a mistake or speak up.

EXERCISE: Social Experiment Log

Experiment 1:
Predicted Outcome:
Actual Outcome:
Reasonable Conclusion:

Experiment 2:
Predicted Outcome:
Actual Outcome:
Reasonable Conclusion:

Experiment 3:
Predicted Outcome:
Actual Outcome:

Reasonable Conclusion:

....

....

Experiment 4:
....
Predicted Outcome:
....
Actual Outcome:
....
Reasonable Conclusion:
....

....

Experiment 5:
....
Predicted Outcome:
....
Actual Outcome:
....
Reasonable Conclusion:
....

....

....

What I am learning from these experiments:

....

....

Repeat!

Anxiety can be a slow learner. If you are worried that people will pounce if you make a little mistake, making a single mistake and observing that the outcome is not catastrophic is unlikely to change that worry significantly.

Therefore, you must repeat your experiments as frequently and with as wide a variety of people as you can. Research shows that doing many experiments in a shorter amount of time provides better results than the same number of experiments spread out over a long period of time. The wider range of people and situations helps generalize the lessons.

LEARNING FROM REJECTION

Gabby

Gabby had been raised to believe that it would be improper for a woman to ask a man on a date. She waited patiently throughout high school and college, but dating just never happened. She had spent most Saturday nights at home watching TV. Still, she kept her spirits up and pushed forward with life. Now she was living in a vibrant new city, having recently been promoted to a position at the corporate office.

This big change had been a grand adventure and she was loving her new life! She had made so many close friends, male and female, and had a very active social life, which boosted her interpersonal confidence dramatically. She found herself attracted to one of her male friends whom she had met five months earlier. She had hoped that he'd ask her out, but he had not. Perhaps he was just shy, she thought, and she decided to take matters into her own hands. She bolstered her confidence and approached him after a dinner party they both attended as they were walking to their cars. She looked him right in the eyes. It was now or never. She took the biggest risk of her social life and said, "I had such a fun time chatting with you tonight, Michael! I was thinking, you and I should hang out, just the two of us. How about we do something fun this weekend?" She held his gaze and smiled, nervously waiting for his reply.

"To be honest, I'm not sure if I'm into us doing the one-on-one thing," he said as he looked away. "Why don't we see if the rest of the gang can join us?"

Gabby was disappointed and a felt a bit embarrassed about being rebuffed. But she also realized that this was not some big traumatic event. Being rejected was not nearly as bad as she had worried it would be. She would live to date another day!

Some people spend their adolescence and early adulthood avoiding asking someone on a date out of fear of rejection. Once they finally behave courageously and ask someone out, they may still end up getting turned down. But, rather than falling apart, they are often amazed that the rejection was not such a terrible blow after all and that they recovered quite quickly. Learning that this dreaded rejection was not so catastrophic gave them additional courage to continue pursuing and eventually succeed at dating.

Yes, you could blush, sweat, appear nervous, and so forth. And, yes, you could be rejected (though the likelihood is probably less than you imagine). Most of us are on the receiving end of at least some rejection from time to time. It is important to determine:

- Is rejection as likely as anxiety has been telling you?
- Is rejection as catastrophic as anxiety has been saying?
- Is the clean discomfort of rejection really so unbearable that it is worth giving up on major social goals?

BUILDING UP YOUR SOCIAL MUSCLES

The social experiments that you conduct with open eyes and an open mind help you to see things for how they really are rather than through the nightmare imagination of the anxious five-year-old inside you. Spoiler alert: You may realize that people are not ready to pounce on you for the slightest social faux paus or imperfection. You may even begin to conclude that social interactions just are not as dangerous as they have felt.

However, this is just a start.

When you learn something new, like how to speak a foreign language or how to play a musical instrument, it will feel strange and awkward at first. Only over time with practice will your skills improve and will the sound flow more smoothly. Interpersonal interactions or social performance endeavors work the same way. When you have been avoiding them or hiding behind safety behaviors, they will feel more awkward and the social skills rusty or under-developed. Rather than beating yourself up over your awkward rustiness, try to see yourself as understandably "out of shape" in those situations. It will take time and practice for those social muscles to develop, but through social "workouts" you can get back in shape socially in those situations.

As often as you can, ask yourself, "What can I do for today's social workout?" Then hit the social gym and push yourself. Allow the anxiety along the way to be a positive discomfort, meaning that you are getting in a good workout.

During these workouts, you also have the opportunity to practice wielding the social-discomfort coping tools that have been discussed in this book. Hone your ability to incorporate mindfulness, acceptance, defusion, and compassion throughout your social exercise. Make those skills part of your daily social experience so they become positive coping habits.

It takes a good defense as well as offense to win the game!

Setting up a social challenge for yourself and carrying it out is your social game's offensive strategy. You are grabbing the social ball and running toward victory. Life, however, will throw additional unplanned challenges your way on a regular basis. Perhaps you are just going about your day, minding your own business when:

- Your boss calls you in for a "chat"
- Your teacher calls on you in class
- You receive a text from an old friend you have not seen in ages
- A few coworkers spring a lunch invitation on you
- Your boss informs you that you've been named employee of the year and will be giving a speech in front of the entire corporate team
- The attractive person at the coffee shop asks you out
- Your church is planning a five-day retreat

- You show up at the party and realize you barely know anyone there

Life is quite likely going to serve up a range of challenging social situations that anxiety will attempt to dissuade you from participating in (or load you up with safety behaviors). Having a good defensive strategy in place means that you err on the side of saying "yes" if for no other reason than because anxiety told you to say "no" and this is a social growth opportunity.

You could take it a step further and play the rule of opposites as your default response to social anxiety. The rule of opposites means that you listen to what anxiety tells you to do and then do the opposite. If there are two checkout lines at the grocery store and anxiety tells you to take the one on the left behind the gentleman quietly staring at his cell phone, then you make the choice to take the one on the right with the Chatty Cathy looking for someone to gab with.

Just begin to notice all of the minor decisions that social anxiety makes for you and begin to specifically go after all those situations that anxiety attempts to influence you away from. Couple this strong defensive strategy with your planned offensive strategy and you have a winning playbook.

Bolster your motivation by frequently reviewing your goals

Regularly review what you wrote earlier in the book about why you want to learn to face your social fears. I work with a lot of college students who need to decide whether to attend the social function that will provide them the opportunity to begin making friends and perhaps a dating partner or whether they will stay in their rooms alone, yet again, and play video games. Anxiety will make a strong case for the lonely night of gaming, so your case for the importance of meeting your social goals has to be much more convincing.

So, keep your eye on the social prizes ahead and put one foot in front of the other and continue moving forward.

TARGETING SOCIAL EXPOSURE THERAPY TO MEET YOUR SOCIAL GOALS

Now let's go beyond basic behavioral experiments and social muscle building and chart a course toward the goals you identified earlier in the book. It is time to put those growing social muscles to work for you. To do this, you will select a target goal, break the goal down into manageable social challenges, and then work up your hierarchy of challenges while rewarding yourself for your efforts along the way.

Let's look at each step.

Step 1. Select a goal

Which goal do you want to start with?

- Pursue friendships
- Go after a romantic relationship
- Get more comfortable or proficient with public speaking
- Increase your assertiveness at home or at work
- Improve your ability to make small talk

Something to consider is whether to pick an easier goal and claim a quicker victory to build up your social confidence. Alternatively, you can select your goal based on what you most desire. You could even select multiple goals to work on simultaneously.

The choice is entirely yours.

My first social goal is:

....

....

Step 2. Break your goal into bite-sized social challenges

There is a well-known phenomenon in graduate school known as All-But-Dissertation (ABD). ABDs are those students who have finished their coursework, but when presented with the task of writing their dissertation (quite a large project), they freeze. These students are so overly focused on completing their dissertation—just having it done—that they cannot focus on the step directly in from of them. One of my colleagues who started graduate school with me actually graduated seven years after I did for this very reason. Some students never go on to complete their dissertation and therefore never graduate.

This can happen anytime we are faced with a lengthy challenge (like writing a book on social courage, for example). Rather than approaching it step by step, some people stop and stare at the entirety of the task ahead and just give up. This happens frequently with social goals as well. If you are contemplating dating or friendship formation after many years of avoidance, this certainly can feel like a daunting challenge. The way out of this procrastination trap is to break the task down into small steps and then keep your eyes on the step right in front of you. Take it one step at a time and continue moving forward in the direction of your goal. Be patient with yourself and with others and just put one foot in front of the other and move.

Let's look at an example.

Jade

Jade was a shy nineteen-year-old beginning her second year at the local state university. She lived at home during her freshman year and would show up on campus just to attend class, then rush home afterward. It was lonely, but she figured that at least she had the company of her parents every evening. Her parents, however, recognized her growing loneliness and budding depression and told her that she must live on campus her sophomore year in order to make friends. She reluctantly agreed.

She never really had any close friends and it felt like an insurmountable hill to climb. She consulted a therapist in the counseling center and together they made the following plan to help her move from shy avoider to socially courageous friend.

Jade's Goal: Behave in ways that increase the likelihood of making friends

Rank	Challenge	Dates Practiced
1	Make eye contact with strangers on campus	
2	Make eye contact with people I know	
3	Smile briefly at strangers on campus	
4	Smile briefly at people I know	
5	Say "Hello" to people in passing	
6	Say "Hello" to people in my classes	
7	Have a brief conversation with a campus store employee	
8	Have a brief conversation with a classmate	
9	Give a compliment to a professor about his or her lecture	
10	Give a compliment to a classmate	
11	Take an interest and learn three things about a classmate	
12	Say "yes" to a social invitation and attend	
13	Join at least one campus club or organization	
14	Attend a social event and introduce yourself to at least three people	
15	Attend a social event and initiate small talk for approximately three minutes with at least three people	
16	Ask other people to form a study group for at least one class	
17	Suggest a fun activity to at least one person for a specific day and time	

Safety behaviors I will not perform while facing my fears:

1. Get drunk or high
2. Stay close to one or two "safe" people
3. Strive to be perfect
4. Remain internally focused

EXERCISE: Your turn! Select a social goal and create a social challenge hierarchy.

Concrete Goal:

Directions: Break the goal down into concrete steps, starting with easiest and working up to more challenging tasks. Please include at the bottom the safety behaviors you are willing to give up during your social exposures.

Rank	Challenge	Dates Practiced

Safety behaviors I will not perform while facing my fears:

1. ....
2. ....
3. ....

Tip: Try not to rigidly focus just on your challenge hierarchy. If other social opportunities present themselves that propel you in the same desired direction, then be flexible enough to go for them.

Step 3. Reward your effort

A basic fact of psychology is that behavior that is rewarded tends to persist or increase while behavior that goes without reward or is punished tends to stay the same or decrease. If you want to build momentum to keep pushing forward with social challenges, I would encourage you to plan to reward yourself following completion of each challenge.

You could simply mentally pat yourself on the back or you could reward yourself externally by watching your favorite show or grabbing takeout at your favorite restaurant. What is important is that you tie your courageous behaviors to a positive reinforcement of some kind.

Nadia

Nadia no longer tried to hide her blushing. She had learned through social experimentation that people did not reject her for blushing. In fact, most people didn't tend to notice and a few people even made endearing comments to her about the attractive red hue that her face took on. Getting to this realization took persistent challenges through social experimentation to anxiety's theory that blushing equals catastrophe.

It had not been easy, though!

In order to bolster her motivation while she did the hard work of daily social challenges, she rewarded herself after each challenge by watching her favorite TV show that evening. Once a week, if she had practiced consistently, she treated herself to a massage.

Step 4. Evaluate your progress

So, let's assume you've been working hard on behaving with more social courage. You've been doing your social experimentation and social-muscle building. During those practices you've engaged a variety of strategies to help you cope and thrive with the scary thoughts and anxious feelings that have naturally arisen. You've selected reasonable social goals (Settling for Duke or Earl rather than aiming for King of England, perhaps). Now the logical question is—how much progress are you making?

Let's try a self-assessment:

- Do you have increasing freedom to make your own decisions regarding social situations rather than anxiety calling the shots? Or, is anxiety still the primary determiner of which social situations you enter and which you avoid?
- Are you better able to live with the reality of some degree of socially anxious feelings as a normal clean discomfort of daily life? Or, are you still running from those feelings, demanding that they forever and completely be banished from your life?
- Are you observing that social rejection has been less frequent and less catastrophic than anxiety has predicted? Are your target social situations beginning to seem less risky than before?
- Perhaps most importantly, are you making observable and measurable progress toward your reasonable social goals?

If you do not feel that you are moving forward in your quest to better cope and thrive with social anxiety and move toward your goals, then keep reading. If you are moving forward at a reasonable pace—keep going!

In the following chapter, we will discuss common obstacles that might interfere with your coping and thriving with social anxiety or in achieving your social goals.

7

Troubleshooting Social Anxiety

*Dealing with setbacks and obstacles
you may encounter along the way*

Lucas

Lucas had always imagined that he'd be comfortably settled into a longstanding marriage by this age. Perhaps their children would be grown and living away at college and he and his wife would have more time for slow cups of coffee in the morning and long walks in the evening. Maybe they'd travel to some of the places he'd always dreamed of visiting.

At nearly fifty years old, however, Lucas found himself filled with feelings of shame and despair for the way things had turned out.

Despite his fantasy of family life, he had never been married. In fact, he had yet to go out on a date—ever. His life consisted of sitting in front of a computer screen during the day and going home after work to his loyal canine companion. At home, he stared at the TV night after night while eating and drinking his loneliness to sleep. The years had briskly skipped along and his romantic dreams had gathered nothing but dust. Now, he feared, it was too late.

At the end of the last chapter, it was very tempting to conclude the book with " … and they lived happily ever after—The End." And then end scene, roll credits, and you happily shuffle out into the bright, shiny social world around you. Well, unfortunately, in the real world, things don't always go so smoothly.

Setbacks are the rule in life, not the exception. Most likely there will be obstacles in the road, blocking you from a social goal. You must do your best to navigate your way around them. You could choose to struggle with this reality, but that would only serve to heap dirty discomfort upon you.

Instead, I recommend that you matter-of-factly acknowledge when there is an obstacle or setback, then shower yourself with self-compassion. It is okay to get stuck—you never have to beat yourself up over having the problems that come along with being human. At times like these, try to shift your focus from frustration or defeat to viewing this as another growth opportunity.

Then, approach the obstacle in front of you as a problem or puzzle to be solved.

PROBLEM SOLVING

When faced with a social problem, you can let it derail you or you can face it head on in a systematic manner. Maybe you are a single parent struggling to even find a moment for yourself, let alone a social life. Perhaps you live with a disability that places limits on your social energy. Maybe a lack of financial resources makes certain desirable social activities unrealistic for you at this time—taking someone to dinner and a movie can cost an arm and a leg these days. Or maybe, as in the case of Lucas, your social progress has grinded to a halt for reasons not immediately apparent to you. By approaching problems or obstacles in a systematic way, you attempt to come up with the best solution or solutions to meet the challenge.

Let's look at a simple formula for solving problems. Then, if needed, you can practice working on a solution to a current problem that might be holding you back from achieving your social goals.

Step 1: Identify a problem that is standing in the way of your social goal attainment.

Make this as specific, rather than judgmental, as you can.

Judgmental	Specific
I am un-datable	I would like to date, but have not yet done so
I am terrible at small talk	I am at a loss for how to talk to people at a party
I'm bad at sticking up for myself	I am not as assertive as I would like to be

Step 2: Brainstorm possible solutions.

Brainstorming is a creative way of generating ideas that can be used to solve a problem. It involves taking your imagination off the leash and directing it toward a specific goal. The rules are simple:

• Write as many ideas for a solution to your problem as you can think of without censoring or judgment.

• Don't dig into the feasibility of any of the possible solutions until you are done. Even outrageous ideas ("Find the perfect man on Mars") may spark another idea that later will turn out to be more feasible ("Join a club for space enthusiasts"). Just keep writing ideas.

Step 3: Pick the top feasible solutions and list the pros and cons for each.

Run through your list and immediately cross out the ideas that are wildly impractical or downright undesirable. If you are unsure of which ones are impractical, you can always ask someone you trust to review the list with you. If you are in doubt as to whether an idea is feasible, feel free to leave it on the list for further exploration.

For each of the possible solutions, make a list of pros and cons. Then, weigh the pros against the cons in order to decide whether to rule out a potential solution. Based on the individual pros and cons, you will either select a single strategy or a combination of strategies.

The actual number of pros and cons for a specific solution doesn't necessarily make it a good or bad option. You could have a solution that has five pros, but only one con, but that one con greatly outweighs the five pros. For example, if one solution is to go skydiving without a parachute, the pros may outnumber the cons, but the one con might be a real knockout!

Skydiving without a parachute

PRO	CON
Exhilarating!	Splat ...
I'll be famous	
Huge thrill	
The views are amazing	

Step 4: Select a solution or combination of solutions and implement.

There is no real way to predict the future with certainty. The best you can do is make an educated guess based on the pros and cons that you have delineated. Ultimately, to move forward, you need to make a choice and get started. If you procrastinate while waiting for a solution that has a one-hundred percent chance of success, then you will never solve the problem. Pick reasonable solutions and act on them. You have every right to make a mistake and then try other solutions. Don't let perfectionism hold you hostage to inactivity.

Step 5: Evaluate the results.

Give the solution you have selected a reasonable amount of time and then take a step back and do an honest assessment of your chosen strategy.

Did your strategy succeed in removing the obstacle that was blocking the path toward your social goals? If the answer is yes, then congratulations on continuing your journey forward. If the answer is no, then either implement another strategy that you came up with in your latest round of brainstorming or return back to Step 1 and proceed again, bringing what you have learned into the second round of problem-solving.

Let's look at the example of Lucas's problem solving. Then it will be your turn to practice.

Solving Lucas's Problem

Step 1: Identify a problem that is standing in the way of your social goal attainment.

I'd like to have a romantic relationship. However ...
I don't know how to act around women. I haven't a clue.
I have tried to meet women online, but after one or two
interactions with them, they never respond again. Even
if they did respond to me, I have no idea how to turn the
interaction into a date. Though if I did get a date, I wouldn't
know how to behave on one.

Step 2: Brainstorm possible solutions.

1. I could try to date older rather than younger women
2. I could try a different dating site, maybe one that you pay for
3. I could change my cologne
4. I could wear a tuxedo to the grocery store
5. I could read up on stylish clothing for men
6. I could win an ultra-marathon
7. I could work with a personal trainer
8. I could drink more
9. I could limit my drinking
10. I could take a break from alcohol
11. I could read about social skills
12. I could watch videos on social skills
13. I could work with a therapist to learn and practice social skills
14. I could just give up!
15. I could create a robot girlfriend
16. I could try to be more patient

17. I could just practice talking with women—no pressure for anything
18. I could hang out with my friends and their wives and practice talking to their wives
19. I could ask female friends for feedback
20. I could try to observe how other people interact with women
21. I could ask my doctor for an antidepressant prescription
22. I could date only supermodels
23. I could lower my perfectionistic standards for dating partners—I'm not perfect either!
24. I could make my home less college dorm-like and more pleasant for adults

Step 3: Pick the top *feasible* solutions and list the pros and cons for each.

Give up		Limit drinking		Dress more stylishly	
PRO	**CON**	**PRO**	**CON**	**PRO**	**CON**
I won't have to change	I don't like my life as it is	I'll save money	It is the only thing that makes me feel good	Some women may like that	I like to dress comfortably
I'll have less anxiety if I don't try to date	It would be sad to give up on something I really want	I'll be healthier	Eases the pain		It will be expensive to get a new wardrobe
	I'll be alone for the rest of my life—I really don't want that!	I'll get out and do more with my life	My friends drink a lot—it won't be fun to hang out with them		I'm only interested in dating someone who likes to be casual

Read about social skills		Work with a therapist		Watch social skills videos	
PRO	**CON**	**PRO**	**CON**	**PRO**	**CON**
It's a proactive approach I can learn a lot this way I can use all the help I can get with social skills	I'll feel ashamed of myself for having to read about what I should already know	The therapist will hold me accountable for making changes and reaching my goal Getting feedback from a neutral party will be helpful Maybe they can help me to drink less and feel less depressed	Time commitment Money commitment I don't want to feel pressured; I'd prefer to go at my own pace I'd really like to try to meet my goal on my own It will be very uncomfortable	I learn better by seeing people demonstrate skills It's free There are probably many videos online to watch	I'll feel silly doing this

Interact with friends' wives		Work with a personal trainer		Lower perfectionistic standards	
PRO	**CON**	**PRO**	**CON**	**PRO**	**CON**
These are the only women I see socially They probably would want to help me	It feels weird and uncomfortable	They will hold me accountable I'll get healthier I'll look better Might increase my confidence	Big time and money commitment Not sure I can stick with it	I don't like being superficial I have been unrealistic This increases my chance to find a romantic match Much larger pool to choose from	I would feel sad to lower my standards I might not feel the same attraction

191

> Step 4: Select a solution or combination of solutions and implement
>
> I will:
> *Begin working with a trainer, read and watch videos on social skills and begin to practice them with my friends' wives, lower my standards on appearance and focus on inner beauty, and get a therapist if I am still stuck after six months.*

EXERCISE: Selecting and solving a problem blocking your social goal

Step 1: Identify a problem that is standing in the way of your social goal attainment.

....

....

....

Step 2: Brainstorm possible solutions.

1.
....
2.
....
3.
....
4.
....
5.
....
6.
....
7.
....
8.
....
9.
....
10.
....
11.
....
12.
....
13.
....

14. ....
15. ....
16. ....
17. ....
18. ....
19. ....
20. ....
21. ....
22. ....
23. ....
24. ....

Additional:

Step 3: Pick the top *feasible* solutions and list the pros and cons for each.

Possible Solution:		Possible Solution:		Possible Solution:	
PRO	CON	PRO	CON	PRO	CON
Possible Solution:		Possible Solution:		Possible Solution:	

PRO	CON	PRO	CON	PRO	CON

Possible Solution:		Possible Solution:		Possible Solution:	

PRO	CON	PRO	CON	PRO	CON

Step 4: Select a solution or combination of solutions and implement.

I will:

....

....

....

....

....

....

I will implement this by the following date: /   /

Step 5: Evaluate the results. Did this solve your problem?

___ YES   ___NO

If yes, congratulations! If no, go back to Step 1.

COMMON PROBLEMS ON THE PATH TO SOCIAL GOAL ATTAINMENT

I am lacking a particular skill needed to achieve my goal

You were born with certain innate drives and reflexes. The rest, however, you have to learn as you go through life. If you spent your youth on a farm in central California, you may find it difficult to navigate the complex social intricacies of corporate culture in the heart of New York City. You would not have developed certain social skills desired in that arena. Likewise, if you were raised in a rough and tumble neighborhood in the heart of New York City, you would lack the understanding of the social particulars needed to integrate into a small farming community (you might experience agriculture shock!). The point being, skills are developed through learning and practice—we are not born with them. So, rather than beating yourself up for being bereft of a specific social or vocational skill, you can assess which skills are lacking and take steps to acquire and practice them.

EXERCISE: Below are examples of common social and vocational skills you may need in order to make progress toward your social goals. Place a checkmark by those skills that would be helpful for you to learn. What resources are available to you to help you learn those skills?

Social Skills
- ☐ Nonverbal interpersonal communication (body language)
- ☐ Verbal interpersonal behavior (rules of thumb for verbal interactions)
- ☐ Small talk

- ☐ Etiquette (local norms of polite behavior)
- ☐ Dressing, grooming, or hygiene
- ☐ Assertiveness (stating what you want directly and respectfully)
- ☐ Friendship formation and maintenance
- ☐ Flirting and dating
- ☐ Other: ....

Vocational Skills
- ☐ Public speaking
- ☐ Leadership/management
- ☐ Study or work skills (how to study, organize, stay focused, and so on)
- ☐ Networking
- ☐ Technical knowledge and skills pertaining to your career

Ways I could learn these skills include: (for example, internet videos, classes, books, coworkers, friends, therapy): ....

....

....

....

....

....

....

....

Underdeveloped skills are not to be confused with inhibited skills. Inhibited skills are those skills that have been learned, but are held back due to anxiety. For example, many of my clients have wonderful small-talk skills that flow smoothly and freely with people whom they know and trust, but become repressed when in certain triggering situations, like meeting someone new at a party. Rather than needing to learn new skills, they may need to practice being more socially courageous using the skills they already have in anxiety-provoking situations.

One additional thing to keep in mind regarding social and vocations skills: they are culture-specific. Many a suave corporate leader has inadvertently offended their counterparts across the globe by following the skills appropriate to their home country that had alternative meanings elsewhere. It makes sense, then, to learn and practice skills that are tailored to those with whom you will be interacting.

It is normal for people in my profession to experience a lot of rejection … and I don't like it!

Social anxiety involves concerns about rejection. With phobic social anxiety, people fear that rejection will be much more likely than what really occurs. For some people, however, significant rejection is part of their daily experience. For example, think of the rejection that comes with the following professions:

- Used-car salesperson
- Parking attendant
- Lawyer
- Telemarketer
- Debt collector
- Politician
- Tax auditor
- Self-help author

All of this rejection can lead to an increase in one's social anxiety levels— or, conversely, it can actually lead to a *decrease* in the daily emotional impact of this rejection. If the rejection is seen as clean discomfort and softly accepted as part of the job, you may build up a tolerance to the rejection over time. If, on the other hand, you pour on the dirty discomfort, hating the rejection and bemoaning your fate, then your anxiety may continue to grow and your sense of suffering is sure to increase, too.

When working in a high-rejection arena, you may also cope better if you prepare ahead of time so that when rejection is hurled your way, you have a prepared response that you can hold your head up high and deliver. ("I'm sorry you feel that way, but I don't write the tax code. Let's try to make the best of this.")

Sometimes, however, if you recognize that your job doesn't suit your personality or social goals, planning a vocational pivot may be the most self-compassionate action you can take.

I do not have time to devote to increasing my social courage

Life can get hectic and sometimes the complexities of our daily lives can interfere with our social goals. I have worked with single parents of multiple children who also work time-consuming and demanding jobs while caregiving for an elderly parent. Free time was not to be found in abundance!

If you truly do not have time at present to make progress toward your social goals, then perhaps the brainstorming session above should revolve around how you might free up time in the future. Are there some lengthy obligations or projects that you could put on hold for a few months? Remember to weigh out your priorities and spend your precious time wisely.

Sometimes multitasking is helpful to make the most of your time. Perhaps you could practice challenging yourself socially in situations that you are already going to be in such as at work or with family. Maybe instead of eating lunch alone at your desk, you could arrange to go to lunch with coworkers.

If you need to slow down your social challenges until you can free up more time, then feel free to do what works for you. Better to take fewer, smaller steps than no steps at all.

I have an addiction or other mental or physical health issue that interferes with my social goals

You can challenge yourself socially even while struggling with other problems. It just makes it more difficult. Take depression. When people are depressed, their motivation to go out into the world and pursue social challenges and goals is like trying to run in a swimming pool. You can get from one side to the other, but with significantly more resistance.

Maybe the first and most important social courage challenge is to speak up and ask for help. Meanwhile, beware of all-or-nothing thinking and move forward at whatever pace you can while addressing interfering concerns.

I cannot find opportunities to challenge myself socially

Seeking social challenges can feel overwhelming if you are accustomed to isolating yourself. Think about all of the places where you could interact with other people—even if it is something you wouldn't normally do. Look for every opportunity.

EXERCISE: If you have had difficulties finding venues to challenge yourself, place a checkmark by all of the ways you could begin to challenge yourself socially.

- ☐ Neighbors
- ☐ People on the bus
- ☐ Place of worship
- ☐ Clubs
- ☐ Volunteering
- ☐ Family
- ☐ Work
- ☐ Toastmasters (for public speaking)
- ☐ Online dating
- ☐ Online meet-ups
- ☐ Become more active on social media
- ☐ Stores or coffee shops
- ☐ Walking your dog
- ☐ Taking a class
- ☐ Old friends or acquaintances you could reconnect with
- ☐ Local singles events
- ☐ Singles group travel
- ☐ Playing a team sport
- ☐ Parents of your children's friends or sports teammates
- ☐ Other: ....

....

....

....

....

....

Take advantage of whatever reasonable opportunities are available to you. Try your best not to search for the perfect people in the perfect situations. This will likely lead to your movement being stalled.

I just hate small talk

I hear this one all the time. When there are "important" things to converse about (global warming, world peace, or the meaning of life and death), why would you want to waste your precious time talking to your cousin Fred about his recent insurance convention in Des Moines? Well, for a couple of reasons. First, small talk is an important way people play and connect with each other. People hanging out and kibitzing at a party are engaged in a time-honored social ritual. It is not about the transfer of information like in a student–teacher interaction, but it is a way of communicating to a person that you value them (at least to some degree) and, consequently, small talk serves to initiate, build, or maintain social relationships. In that sense, the small stuff is the big stuff.

Another reason to embrace the ritual of small talk is that it is a pathway to deeper conversation. As they say, small talk is the grease on the wheels of more meaningful communication. You've got to start with basic pleasantries before transitioning to the meatier issues. It wouldn't be socially appropriate, for example, to approach someone at a party and say, "Hi, I'm Eric! What do you think about the impact of global warming on world peace?" In time, small talk can blossom into more profound discussions.

Try to approach small talk lightly and playfully. Focus on the process rather than getting bogged down in the content. Think about the message behind chatting with your great aunt Sandra about her knee replacement surgery or schmoozing with Betty from Accounting about her recent trip to Kalamazoo. By taking part in the small talk social ritual, you are communicating well beyond the topic being tossed back and forth. Underneath the surface, you are transmitting other messages all together such as, "I like you." "I am happy you are part of the family." "Let's play." "I'm not a threat and don't see you as one either." "I'm attracted to you." "I'm really happy to spend time with you." And so on.

From this perspective, there is no small talk. There is only a lack of understanding of the broader messages behind the content.

In addition to the greater meaning behind small talk, keep in mind that these "small" interactions are your social skills training grounds. Each interpersonal encounter provides you the opportunity to practice sharpening your social skills and social courage strategies.

People constantly disappoint me

If you demand social perfection from yourself, you will consistently fail to meet your expectations. Likewise, if you impose unreasonably high expectations on your fellow humans, you will consistently feel let down by them. Just like you and I make social mistakes, others will as well. No one is immune from occasional flare-ups of foot-in-mouth disease.

We are all flawed creatures. That will never change. Rather than living with the fantasy that you will someday discover and join the lost continent of perfect humans, try to feel compassion for others (and yourself) as we go about living out our imperfect lives the best way we can.

Sometimes people feel that they are putting more work into maintaining a relationship than their friends or family members. If you think about it, though, what are the odds that a relationship will consist of a perfect fifty–fifty split in the effort to maintain it? Seems highly unlikely that interpersonal give and take will ever be completely equal in any relationship. You might be a higher-than-average person when it comes to social graces and interpersonal effort while others might be merely average in those respects.

Rather than bemoaning the inadequacies of human relationships (and thus layering on dirty discomfort), how about treating others in a way that is consistent with your value system and lowering your expectation for others? Be the attentive friend because that is the kind of person you would like to be, rather than expecting completely equal effort from others in return. Savor what you can from relationships rather than tossing them aside for their imperfections.

On the other hand, if you are experiencing abuse in a relationship, then explore concrete steps toward your own well-being. Life is too short to spend your social and emotional resources on people who persistently tear you down.

I just don't believe anything can help me ... It feels hopeless

This sounds like perhaps depression is blocking your move forward. Or, maybe you have a long history of social avoidance and the prospect of climbing out of the avoidance hole seems overwhelming.

I'd recommend that you accept the presence of these thoughts and feelings and keep moving forward toward your social goals, even at a very casual pace. Consistency is key. If you feel like giving up completely, then your first act of social courage may be to contact a licensed psychotherapist to help keep you moving forward while dealing with obstacles such as depression.

You may be dealing with phobic social anxiety. My experience with phobias is that most people who are dealing with a phobia of clinical proportions have serious doubts as to whether they could ever directly face their fear, whether it be flying in a plane, interacting with a spider, riding in an elevator, or asking someone out on a date. Your sense of impossibility is normal, but your phobic social anxiety is treatable, even if it doesn't feel like it. You just need to make moving forward a priority and keep putting one foot in front of the other. Take it one step at a time.

My goal needs to be modified

The measure of intelligence is the ability to change.

Albert Einstein

I met someone recently who was in great distress. She had fantasized her entire life about becoming a full-time writer. She had imagined herself basking in the peaceful solitude of her home office, day after day joyfully spewing forth creative material onto each new blank page. One day, this person happily quit her stable nine-to-five and followed her dream of becoming a writer. Reality, however, rudely intruded upon her happy fantasy. Soon after announcing to her family and friends that she was now a professional writer, she was faced with the profoundly disappointing realization that she hated writing. She began to fill up her lonely days at home with an endless barrage of internet distractions, wishing her reality would match up with her long-held fantasy.

It can be difficult to revise a goal that you may have devoted significant time and energy to pursuing. Maybe the goal you have selected is tied to a cherished self-perception. I have worked with a number of mechanical engineering majors who are really excited about one day becoming an "engineer" (and the financial perks that come with it) but are utterly repulsed by the scientific and mathematical barrage of learning requirements that comes with such a career path.

If you are in such a situation, try being self-compassionate. It is okay to make a decision and then change your mind and chart a new course when the reality of your decision turns out very differently than you expected. At other times, however, the goal you have may be modified rather than completely abandoned. For example:

- Instead of striving for the supermodel on TV, perhaps you could flirt with that nice person from church who brought you soup when you were ill.
- Instead of setting an educational goal of Harvard or bust, perhaps you could pursue an educational path at another fine institution.
- Instead of planning to become President of the United States, perhaps you could run for president of your local parent–teacher association.

What is important is that rather than getting hung up on a particular goal, you determine what the values behind the goals are (love, education, and leadership) and focus on modifying your goals so that they are achievable and in line with your current values system.

But I don't know what my values are, so I don't know which goals to set

Occasionally, people with social anxiety may be aware that they are missing out or are lonely, but not really sure which social goals they want to set for themselves. Spending time thinking about what is truly most important to you in life—your values—can help illuminate desired social goals.

EXERCISE: If you are unsure of which road you wish social courage to take you down, then consider the following values clarification exercises to help illuminate what is truly important to you.

Close your eyes and imagine the following:

1. Many years from now, you are at the end of your life— and it was a life well lived. Looking back through this life, what was most meaningful for you in terms of relationships, activities, and accomplishments?

....

....

....

....

....

2. Your doctor tells you that you have five years left to live. The good news is that you will feel remarkably great during that time. You will have a lot of energy, motivation, and confidence. Social anxiety will not be a limiting factor. How will you spend this time and with whom?

....

....

....

....

....

....

3. If you could send an email to yourself ten years ago,
    what would you advise the younger you to do differently
    regarding social avoidance and social courage? What
    would you want your past self to do differently?

....

....

....

....

....

....

4. You receive an email from the socially courageous you
    from ten years in the future, giving you an update on your
    life and advising you regarding people, relationships, and
    cherished activities. How might that email read?

....

....

....

....

....

....

What values do your answers reflect?

For example:

- Friendships
- Romantic Relationship
- Family
- Achievement
- Financial
- Spiritual
- Health
- Inner Peace
- Nature

....
....
....
....
....
....

How might those values translate into specific social or vocational goals?

For example:

Value	Social Goals
Friendships	Increase number of friendships Increase depth of friendships
Romantic Relationship	Be in a committed romantic relationship
Family	Spend more time with parents Improve relationship with siblings Develop a closer relationship with your children
Achievement/ Financial	Go back to college and earn a degree Ask for a raise at work Interview for a new job Improve public speaking and networking skills

Spiritual	Join and speak up at a bible study group
	Attend place of worship regularly
	Join a meditation group
Health	Exercise regularly at a gym
	Take an exercise class
	Join a hiking club
Inner Peace	Join a yoga class
	Attend a personal growth retreat
Nature	Take a singles' vacation to the Caribbean
	Participate in a nature cleanup organization
	Invite people to go on hikes outdoors

List your top values and possible social goals derived from those values.

Value	Social Goals

Now that your social goals are more clearly delineated, set them in your sights and start moving toward them, step by step. Don't look back until you get there.

The Courage to be Human

Final thoughts on social courage

When you are working hard and making progress on the social courage road, make sure to pat yourself on the back along the way. Just think how much easier it would have been to just continue avoiding uncomfortable social situations. By pushing beyond the temporary gratification of avoidance and moving forward into the heart of your social discomfort, you have taken a huge step toward achieving your social goals.

Social anxiety is a normal part of life, so the goal is more peaceful coexistence with the anxiety rather than struggling to eliminate this emotion. If the social avoidance slowly begins to ratchet back up in your life and you find yourself again moving away from your social goals, remind yourself that occasional lapses are normal. Approach these lapses with compassion and try to learn from them. Then get back on the social horse and head back out to greener social pastures.

While you have reached the end of this book, I hope this is the beginning of a life where you are neither controlled by social anxiety nor suffer excessively in its presence. When I run social courage groups or retreats, we traditionally have one final social challenge before declaring victory and adjourning for the last time. We break out the karaoke machine (*Oh, the horror!*) and each member takes a turn up in front of the group belting out a Beatles song into the microphone.

This challenge represents something that at the beginning would have felt so socially terrifying that no participant would have ever truly thought they would be able to take part in such a spotlight-grabbing act—in public. Once they have completed this final challenge, however, they then know that no matter how scary a social challenge life tosses their way, they have the ability to push themselves far beyond what they ever considered possible—and live to tell the tale. They feel free.

In the end, however, they and you will remain a human being. Despite the promises from gurus everywhere that you can achieve ultimate transcendence from anxiety, you will continue to experience anxiety at times. You are forever destined to be and feel imperfect—just like the rest of us. The courage to be human lies in recognizing that fact, giving up the impossible quest for perfection, and moving forward anyway—just doing the best you can and seeing that most of the time it is good enough.

Best wishes to you in all your social endeavors now and in the future.

Eric Goodman

ACKNOWLEDGMENTS

The seeds for *Social Courage* were sown back when I was training to become a psychologist at the Edith Nourse Rogers Memorial Veterans Hospital in Bedford, Massachusetts.

My first supervisor and mentor there was Ed Federman. He instilled in me a love for the concrete, research-based, hands-on approach of cognitive-behavioral therapy. He also showed me that if we can help clients approach life with a bit of humor, then treatment and rapport are enhanced.

Two more of my supervisors, the "two Jims" (Jim Schuele and Jim Lindsley), regularly picked apart my clinical work to keep my approach laser-targeted on the client's problems with treatment approaches that were empirically-based (I couldn't get away with making things up!).

They introduced me to the writings and concepts of Aaron Beck, Albert Ellis, David Burns, and David Barlow—each a master of cognitive-behavioral therapy. I was sold and became a card-carrying member of the cognitive-behavioral therapists. I was going to teach people how to think more adaptively and cure their various pathologies!

Over time, however, I began to notice that "changing" maladaptive thoughts did not stop them. I could help people to see things in a new light ("Wow, maybe rejection might not be so catastrophic after all!") which was helpful, but people's impish monkey minds continued to warn of imminent doom. I also came to the realization that although targeting symptom reduction was a helpful for clients, life would continue to provide a buffet of human discomfort.

Then Ed retired and there was a new director of training—Richard Amodio. Richard was not a cognitive-behavior therapist. He had this strange "new" way of approaching unpleasant thoughts and emotions. Rather than trying to challenge them, he was a proponent of sitting with them without judging them. "Heresy!" I thought initially, but over time I grew to understand the power of letting go of trying to control thoughts and permanently vanquish unpleasant emotions.

I was introduced to the concepts of Buddhism, not as a religion, but as a brilliant system of psychology. This led me to finding other great teachers and writings from the likes of Steven Hayes and his ground-breaking work known as acceptance and commitment therapy, Viktor Frankl and his work on living a meaningful life given the reality of pain, and Paul Gilbert, Kristin Neff, and Lynne Henderson and their works on infusing compassion into psychotherapy.

I feel profound gratitude to each of these teachers for their concepts and approaches to helping people. They have shaped me professionally and personally in ways that can't be overstated.

But which teacher and system of psychology was the "right" one?

Some purists representing these great therapy traditions want people to make a choice; for example, you can be a traditional cognitive-behavioral therapist or you can be an acceptance and commitment therapist. You can work to challenge thoughts and reduce anxiety or work to accept thoughts and move forward with your life, anxiety in tow.

Jim #2 (Lindsley) taught me to care less about allegiance to a particular guru or therapy and care more about having empirically-based tools to give to my clients in order to help make their lives better. Joseph Ciarrochi's work on "bridging the gap" between traditional CBT and ACT helped give me the courage to attempt a merger of multiple well-established strategies in a way that emphasizes the strengths of each.

Clinicians, like myself, have the good fortune to be able to reap the benefits of the meticulous work done by a variety of researchers, while not needing to choose sides. *Social Courage* is an integration of concepts that are research-based, fit well together theoretically, and have been useful clinically.

The biggest inspirations for this book are my clients and workshop participants over the years. The fact that your brain screams danger at the thought of negative judgment and yet you show the courage to ask for help and then face your fears directly often leaves me in awe. You are among the most courageous people I know.

Several people were kind enough to read the *Social Courage* manuscript: Dawn Okel, Ellen Pitrowski, and Lynne Henderson. Thank you for your feedback and encouragement.

Thank you to Anouska Jones and the good people at Exisle Publishing, as well as my editor, Yitka Winn. You understood the message that I wanted to convey in *Social Courage* as demonstrated by the fact that you never even suggested adding the snazzy (but impossible) marketing words "Cure" or "Easy Steps" or "Get rid of" in the title— and best of all, you were a lot of fun to work with!

BIBLIOGRAPHY AND RELATED RECOMMENDED READINGS

Chapter 1: Social Anxiety Is Normal

Cain, S. (2012). *Quiet: The Power of Introverts in a World That Can't Stop Talking.* New York: Crown Publishers.

Czeisler, C. A. (2013). Perpective: Casting light on sleep deficiency. *Nature.* doi:doi:10.1038/497S13a

DeYoung, C. G. (2013). The neuromodulator of exploration: A unifying theory of the role of dopamine in personality. *Frontier of Human Neuroscience.* doi:10.3389/fnhum.2013.00762

Dias, B. G., & Ressler, K. J. (2014). Parental olfactory experience influences behavior and neural structure in subsequent generations. *Nature Neuroscience, 17,* 89–96.

Gilbert, P. (2001). Evolution and social anxiety. *Psychiatric Clinics, 24(4),* 723–751.

Newman, J. P. (1997). Conceptual models of the nervous system. In D. M. Stoff, J. Brieling, & J. D. Masers, *Handbook of antisocial behavior* (pp. 324–335). New York: John Wiley and Sons, Inc.

Nieto, S. J., Patriquin, M. A., & Kosten, T. A. (2016). Don't worry; be informed about the epigenetics of anxiety. *Pharmacological Biochemistry Behavior Journal, 146–147,* 60–72.

Owen, N., Healy, G. N., Matthews, C. E., & Dunston, D. W. (2010). Too much sitting: The population-health science of sedentary behavior. *Exercise Sports Science Review, 38(3),* 105–113.

Primack, B. A., Shensa, A., Escobar-Viera, C., Barrett, E. L., Sidani, J. E., Colditz, J. B., & James, A. E. (2017). Use of social media platforms and symptoms of depression and anxiety: A nationally-representative study among U.S. adults. *Computers in Human Behavior, 69,* 1–9.

Slater, A., & Tiggemann, M. (2014). Media matters for boys too! The role of specific magazine types and television programs in the drive for thinness and muscularity in adolescent boys. *Eating Behaviors, 15(4),* 679–682.

Chapter 2: When Normal Anxiety Turns Phobic

Barlow, D. (2002). *Anxiety and its disorders (2nd Edition).* New York: The Guilford Press.

Cambell-Sills, L., Barlow, D. H., Brown, T. A., & Hoffmann, S. G. (2006). Effects of suppression and acceptance on emotional responses of individuals with anxiety and mood disorders. *Behavior Research and Therapy, 44(9),* 1251–1263.

Furmark, T. (2002). Phobia overview of community surveys. *Acta Psychiatrica Scandinavica, 150,* 433–439.

Kessler, R. C., Chiu, W. T., Demler, O., & Walters, M. S. (2005). Prevalence, severity, and co-morbidity of 12-month DSM-IV disorders in the national co-morbidity survey replication. *Archives of General Psychiatry, 62(6),* 617–627.

Mesri, N. B., Pittig, L. R., Haik, E., & Craske, M. E. (2017). Public speaking avoidance as a treatment moderator for social anxiety disorder. *Journal of Behavior Therapy and Experimental Psychiatry, 55*, 66–72.

Neff, K. (2011). *Self-Compassion: The Proven Power of Being Kind to Yourself.* New York: HarperCollins Publishers.

Schneier, F. R., Heckelman, L. R., Garfinkel, R., Campeas, R., Fallon, B., Gitow, A., Liebowitz, M. E. (1994). Functional impairment in social phobia. *Journal of clinical psychiatry, 55*, 322–333.

Schneier, F. R., Hornig, C. D., Liebowitz, M. R., & Weissman, M. M. (1992). Social Phobia: Comorbidity and morbidity in an epidemiological sample. *Archives of General Psychiatry, 49*, 282–288.

Tirch, D. (2012). *The Compassionate-Mind Guide to Overcoming Anxiety: Using Compassion-Focused Therapy to Calm Worry, Panic, and Fear.* Oakland: New Harbinger Publications.

Wang, P. S., Lane, M., Pincus, H. A., Wells, K. B., & Kessler, R. C. (2005). Twelve month use of mental health services in the United States. *Archives of General Psychiatry, 62(6)*, 629–640.

Chapter 3: Cognitive-Behavioral Therapy 2.0

Arch, J. J., & Craske, M. G. (2008). Acceptance and commitment therapy and cognitive behavioral therapy for anxiety disorders: Different treatments, similar mechanisms? *Clinical Psychology: Science and Practice, 15(4)*, 263–279.

Barrera, T. L., & Szafranski, D. D. (2016). An experimental comparison of techniques: Cognitive defusion, cognitive restructuring, and in-vivo exposure. *Behavioural and Cognitive Psychotherapy, 44*, 249–254.

Beck, J. (2011). *Cognitive Behavior Therapy (2nd Edition).* New York: The Guilford Press.

Ciarrochi, J. V., & Bailey, A. (2008). *A CBT Practitioner's Guide to ACT: How to Bridge the Gap Between Cognitive Behavioral Therapy and Acceptance and Commitment Therapy.* Oakland: New Harbinger Publications.

Deacon, B. J., Fawzy, T. I., Likel, J. J., & Wolitsky-Taylor, K. B. (2011). Cognitive defusion versus cognitive restructuring in the treatment of negative self-referential thoughts: An investigation of process and outcome. *Journal of Cognitive Psychotherapy, 25(3)*, 218–232.

Hancock, K., & Swain, J. (2016). Long term follow up in children with anxiety disorders treated with acceptance and comittment therapy or cognitive behavioral therapy. *Journal of Child and Adolescent Behavior, 4(5)*, 317–330.

Hayes, S. C. (2008). Climbing our hills: A beginning conversation on the comparison of acceptance and commitment therapy and traditional cognitive behavior therapy. *Clinical Psychology: Science and Practice, 15(4)*, 286–295.

Hayes, S. C., & Smith, S. (2005). *Get Out of Your mind and into Your Life: The New Acceptance and Commitment Therapy.* Oakland: New Harbinger Publications.

Heimberg, R. G., & Ritter, M. R. (2008). Cognitive behavioral therapy and acceptance and commitment therapy for anxiety disorders: Two approaches with much to offer. *Clinical Psychology: Science and Practice, 15(4)*, 296–298.

Hofman, S. G. (2008). Acceptance and commitment therapy: New wave or morita therapy? *Clinical Psychology: Science and Practice, 15(4)*, 280–285.

Hofman, S. G., & Asmundson, G. J. (2008). Acceptance and mindfulness-based therapy: New wave or old hat? *Clinical Psychology Review, 28(1)*, p. 1–16.

Hofman, S. G., Sawyer, A. T., & Fang, A. (2010). The empirical status of the "new wave" of CBT. *Psychiatric Clinics of North America, 40(2)*, 701–710.

Chapter 4: Brain Noise

Arch, J. J., Wolitzky-Taylor, K. B., Eifert, G. H., & Craske, M. G. (2012). Longitudinal treatment mediation of traditional cognitive behavioral therapy and acceptance and commitment therapy for anxiety disorders. *Behaviour Research and Therapy, 50*(7-8), 469–478.

Beck, A. T., Emery, G., & Greenberg, R. L. (1985). *Anxiety Disorders and Phobias.* New York: Basic Books.

Ellis, A. (1998). *How to Control Your Anxiety Before It Controls You.* New York: Citadel Press.

Fleming, J. E., & Kocovski, N. L. (2013). *The Mindfulness and Acceptance Workbook for Social Anxiety and Shyness.* Oakland: New Harbinger Publications.

Flett, G. L., & Hewitt, P. L. (2002). *Perfectionism: Theory, Research, and Treatment.* Washington, DC: American Psychological Association.

Henderson, L. (2011). *Building Social Confidence: Using Compassion-Focused Therapy to Overcome Shyness and Social Anxiety.* Oakland: New Harbinger Publications.

Hope, D. A., Heimberg, R. G., & Turk, C. L. (2006). *Managing Social Anxiety: A Cognitive-Behavioral Approach (Therapist Guide).* New York: Oxford University Press.

Stoddard, J. A., & Afari, N. (2014). *The Big Book of ACT Metaphors: A Practitioner's Guide to Experiential Exercises and Metaphors in Acceptance and Commitment Therapy.* Oakland: New Harbinger Publications.

Wilson, R. (2009). *Don't Panic.* New York: Harper Perennial.

Chapter 5: Clean vs. Dirty Social Discomfort

Davis, M., Eshelman, E. R., & McKay, M. (1995). *The Relaxation and Stress Reduction Workbook.* Oakland: New Harbinger Publications.

Eifert, G. H., & Forsyth, J. P. (2005). *Acceptance and Commitment Therapy for Anxiety Disorders: A Practitioner's Treatment Guide to Using Mindfulness, Acceptance, and Values-Based Behavior Change Strategies.* Oakland: New Harbinger Publications.

Kabat-Zinn. (2013). *Full Catastrophe Living: Using the Wisdom of Your Body and Mind to Face Stress, Pain, and Illness (Revised Edition).* New York: Bantam Books.

Lejeune, C. (2007). *The Worry Trap: How to Free Yourself from Worry and Anxiety Using Acceptance and Commitment Therapy.* Oakland: New Harbinger Publications.

Stein, M. B., Liebowitz, M. R., Lydiard, B. R., Pitts, C. D., Bushnell, W., & Gergel, I. (1998). Paroxetine treatment for generalized social phobia (social anxiety disorder): A randomized controlled trial. *JAMA, 280(8)*, 708–713.

Chapter 6: Leaving Your Social Comfort Zone

Abramowitz, J. S., Deacon, B. J., & Whiteside, W. P. (2011). *Exposure Therapy for Anxiety.* New York: The Guilford Press.

Barrera, T. L., & Szafranski, D. D. (2016). An experimental comparison of techniques: Cognitive defusion, cognitive restructuring, and in-vivo exposure. *Behavioural and Cognitive Psychotherapy, 44*, 249–254.

Fang, A., Sawyer, A. T., Asnaani, A., & Hofman, S. G. (2013). Social mishap exposures for social anxiety disorder: An important treatment ingredient. *Cognitive and Behavioral Practice, 20(2)*, 213–220.

Henderson, L. (2007). *Social Fitness Training: A Cognitive Behavioral Protocol for the Treatment of Shyness and Social Anxiety.* Palo Alto: Shyness Institute.

Henderson, L. (2014). *Helping Your Shy and Socially Anxious Client: A Social Fitness Training Protocol Using CBT.* Oakland: New Harbinger Publications.

Chapter 7: Troubleshooting Social Anxiety

Harris, R. (2013). *Getting Unstuck in ACT: A Clinician's Guide to Overcoming Common Obstacles in Acceptance and Commitment Therapy.* New York: New Harbinger Publications.

Hilliard, E. B. (2005). *Living Fully with Shyness and Social Anxiety.* Cambridge: Da Capo Press.

Hofman, S. G., & Otto, M. W. (2008). *Cognitive Behavioral Therapy for Social Anxiety: Evidence-Based and Disorder Specific Treatment Techniques.* New York: Routledge.

Markway, B. G., Carmin, C. N., Pollard, C. A., & Flynn, T. (1992). *Dying of Embarrassment.* Oakland: New Harbinger Publications.

Tessina, T. (1998). *The Unofficial Guide to Dating Again.* New York: Wiley Publishing.

Index

technological stimulation, 30
temperament, 24–25
the seducer, Anxiety as, 117–18
thought categories, logical responses, 95–96
thought exposure, 121–22
"thought vendors", 108–9
thoughts
    accepting presence of, 109–10
    are not facts, 54–55
    common types of, 80–86
    coping and thriving with, 126
    don't stop, 106–7
    guru's disagreement, 79–80
    "if only", 94
    logical challenges to, 86–96
    naming the category, 124
    normalizing, 123
    not accepted, 61–62
    observing and accepting, 55, 111
    options for dealing with, 78–79
    personifying, 115–19
    skills for dealing with, 78
    spiritual approach, 114–15
    turn out to be true?, 106
    welcoming, 122
    wishful, 85
time management, 198
triggers, interpretation of, 41–42
Trog and Grog, 23
tug-of-war (anxiety game), 123–24

U
uncertainty-tolerance workout, 57
unfair comparisons, 84, 94, 96

V
values, identifying yours, 204–5
vocational skills, 196

W
wedding speech nerves, 17
wishful thinking, 85
wishing ritual, 94–95, 96
workplace façade, Sarah's, 71–72

31192021525090